Presentations
with PowerPoint

Learning Made Simple

Moira Stephen

ELSEVIER

AMSTERDAM • BOSTON • HEIDELBERG • LONDON • NEW YORK • OXFORD
PARIS • SAN DIEGO • SAN FRANCISCO • SINGAPORE • SYDNEY • TOKYO

Butterworth-Heinemann is an imprint of Elsevier

Butterworth-Heinemann is an imprint of Elsevier
Linacre House, Jordan Hill, Oxford OX2 8DP, UK
30 Corporate Drive, Suite 400, Burlington, MA 01803, USA

First edition 2006

Notice
No responsibility is assumed by the publisher for any injury and/or
damage to persons or property as a matter of products liability,
negligence or otherwise, or from any use or operation of any methods,
products, instructions or ideas contained in the material herein.

TRADEMARKS/REGISTERED TRADEMARKS
Computer hardware and software brand names mentioned in this book
are protected by their respective trademarks and are acknowledged

British Library Cataloguing in Publication Data
A catalogue record for this book is available from the British Library

ISBN-13: 978 0 7506 8188 8
ISBN-10: 0 7506 8188 9

Typeset by P.K. McBride

Icons designed by Sarah Ward © 1994

Printed and bound in Italy

Contents

Preface

The books in the Learning Made Simple series aim to do exactly what it says on the cover – make learning simple.

A Learning Made Simple book:

◆ Is **fully illustrated**: with clearly labelled screenshots.

◆ Is **easy to read**: with brief explanations, and clear instructions.

◆ Is **task-based**: each short section concentrates on one job at a time.

◆ **Builds knowledge**: ideas and techniques are presented in the right order so that your understanding builds progressively as you work through the book.

◆ Is **flexible**: as each section is self-contained, if you know it, you can skip it.

The books in the Learning Made Simple books series are designed with learning in mind, and so do not directly follow the structure of any specific syllabus – but they do cover the content. This book covers Module 6 of the ECDL syllabus and Unit 5 of New CLAIT. For details of how the sections map against your syllabus, please go to the website:

http://www.madesimple.co.uk

1 Getting Started

What is PowerPoint?

PowerPoint is a presentation graphics package. If you have to make presentations, PowerPoint can help make your life easier by giving you the tools that you need to produce your own presentation materials with little or no help from presentation graphics specialists.

You can use PowerPoint to produce:

Slides

Slides are the individual pages of your presentation. They may contain text, graphs, clip art, tables, drawings, animation, movies, music, shapes – and more!! PowerPoint will allow you to present your slides via a slide show on your computer, 35mm slides or overhead projector transparencies.

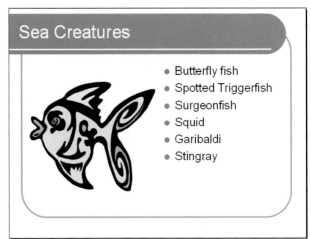

Notes Page

A speaker's notes page accompanies each slide you create. Each notes page contains a small image of the slide plus any notes that you type in. You can print the pages and use them to prompt you during your presentation.

Take note

A PowerPoint presentation is a collection of slides, with optional, but useful support materials, e.g. speaker's notes, handouts and an outline – all in one file.

Handouts

Handouts consist of smaller, printed versions of your slides that can be printed 1, 2, 3, 4, 6 or 9 slides to a page. They provide useful backup material for your audience and can easily be customized with your company name or logo.

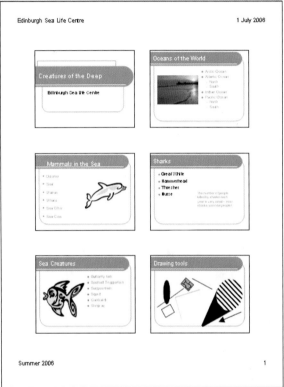

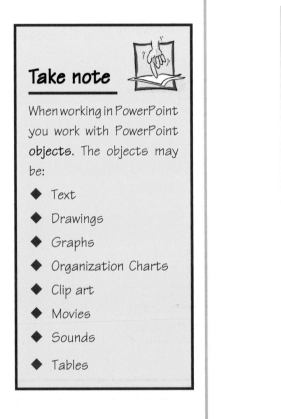

Outline

A presentation Outline contains the slide titles and main text items, but no graphics, WordArt or captions. The Outline gives a useful overview of your presentation's structure.

Starting PowerPoint

Start PowerPoint from the Start menu – in the same way as all other applications.

Basic steps

1 Click the **Start** button

2 Point to **All Programs**

3 Point to **Microsoft Office**

4 Click **Microsoft Office PowerPoint 2003**

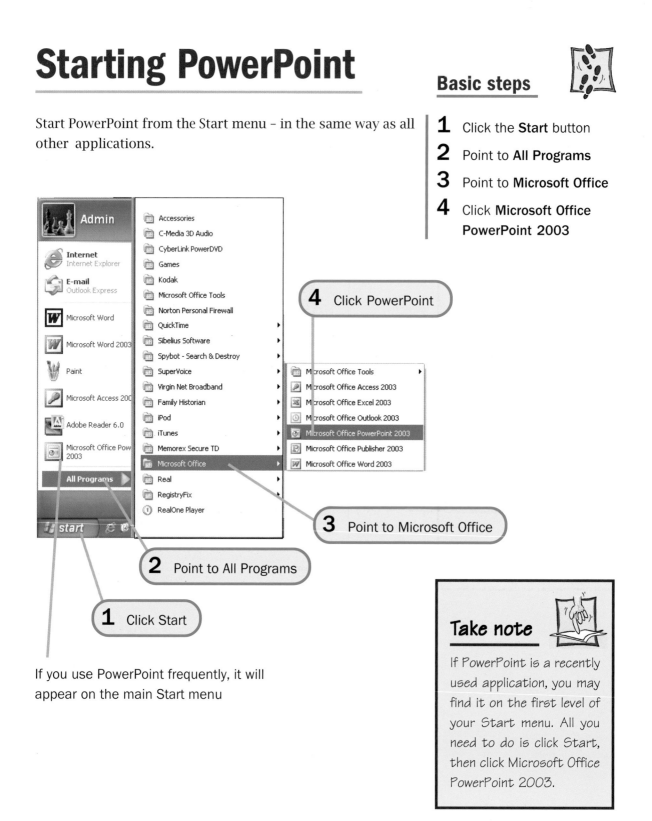

4 Click PowerPoint

3 Point to Microsoft Office

2 Point to All Programs

1 Click Start

If you use PowerPoint frequently, it will appear on the main Start menu

Take note

If PowerPoint is a recently used application, you may find it on the first level of your Start menu. All you need to do is click Start, then click Microsoft Office PowerPoint 2003.

4

The PowerPoint window

Basic steps

- **To control the Standard and Formatting toolbars**

1 Click the **Toolbar Options** button

2 Select **Show Buttons on One Row** or **Two Rows**

- **To display/hide toolbars**

3 Open the **View** menu, choose **Toolbars** then select or deselect the toolbars as required

The PowerPoint window is very similar to other Microsoft applications windows. If you use Word, Excel or Access you will recognise some of the tools on the toolbars.

The Standard and Formatting toolbars usually appear along the top of the window. These two can share a single row on the screen, to leave more room for your work. The Drawing toolbar is usually along the bottom of the window.

The toolbars can be hidden or shown as required.

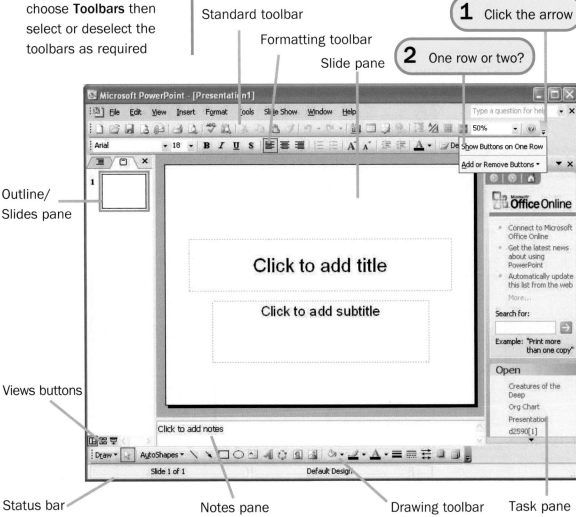

Standard toolbar

Formatting toolbar

Slide pane

1 Click the arrow

2 One row or two?

Outline/ Slides pane

Views buttons

Status bar

Notes pane

Drawing toolbar

Task pane

Normal view

When working on a presentation, you will usually work in Normal view, where the slide takes up most of the screen. There may also be a Outline/Slides pane down the left of the screen with a tab displaying miniature slides and a tab displaying the slide text only in an outline. There is also a notes pane below the slide.

Initially, the Getting Started task pane is displayed on the right of the screen – other task panes will be displayed in this area as you work on your presentation.

You can easily toggle the display of these areas.

Basic steps

- **To hide the panes**

1 Click the ⊠ button on the Outline/Slides pane

- **To restore the panes**

2 Click 🖳 the **Normal (Restore Panes)** tool

or

3 Choose **Normal (Restore Panes)** from the **View** menu

- **To hide the task pane**

4 Click its **Close** button ⊠

- **To display the task pane**

5 Open the **View** menu and choose **Task Pane**

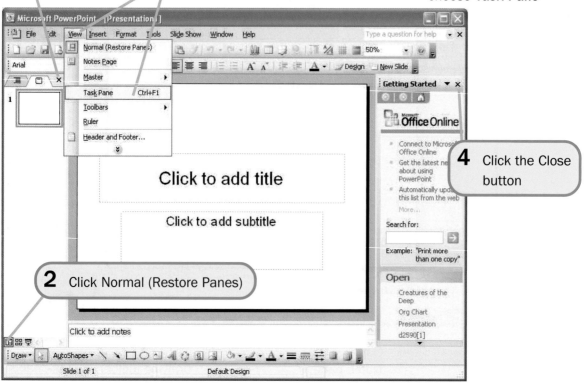

1 Click the Close button

5 Use View > Task Pane

4 Click the Close button

2 Click Normal (Restore Panes)

Basic steps

1 Click the drop-down arrow at the top of the task pane

2 Select the task pane required from the list

Task panes

When you start PowerPoint the Getting Started task pane is displayed on the right-hand side of the screen. As you work with PowerPoint you will find that different task panes appear automatically in this area. You can also select the task pane that you want from the Task Pane list.

Take note

To toggle the display of the task pane press [Ctrl]-[F1].

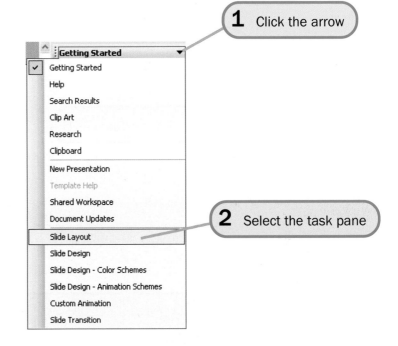

1 Click the arrow

Getting Started

✓ Getting Started
Help
Search Results
Clip Art
Research
Clipboard

New Presentation
Template Help
Shared Workspace
Document Updates

Slide Layout

Slide Design
Slide Design - Color Schemes
Slide Design - Animation Schemes
Custom Animation
Slide Transition

2 Select the task pane

Magnification/Zoom

You can change the magnification/zoom for the Outline tab, the Slides tab, or the slide that's displayed in the slide pane.

If you adjust the magnification for the slide pane, select **Fit** from the Zoom options to display the whole slide again.

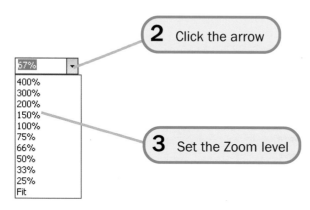

2 Click the arrow

3 Set the Zoom level

1 Click in the area you want to change the magnification of

2 Click the down arrow to display the **Zoom** options (Standard toolbar)

3 Select the magnification from the drop-down list

Take note

Office 2003 applications personalise your menus and toolbars automatically, adding the items that you use most often to them. At first, menus only show the most common commands, though they can be expanded to reveal them all by clicking on the double-arrow at the bottom. After you select a command, it appears on your personalised menu.

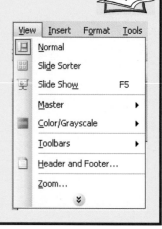

Basic steps

1 Click on a slide on the Slides pane

Or

2 Drag the scroll bar slider. The slide number and title appear as you drag. When you let go of the mouse, the slide appears

Or

3 Click the **Previous Slide** button to move up

4 Click the **Next Slide** button to move down

Moving between slides

There are several ways of moving from one slide to another in your presentation when you are in Normal view.

> ### Keyboard shortcuts
>
> Press [Page Up] to move to the previous slide
>
> [Page Down] to move to the next slide

Microsoft PowerPoint - [Creatures of the Deep]

File Edit View Insert Format Tools Slide Show Window Help

Type a question for help

Arial 24 **B** *I* U S

Design New Slide

1 Click on the slide

ammals in the Sea

Slide: 5 of 10
Sea Creatures

2 Drag the slider

- Dolphin
- Seal
- Walrus
- Whale
- Sea Otter
- Sea Cow

3 Click Previous Slide

4 Click Next Slide

Discuss statistics on populations.

Draw AutoShapes

Slide 3 of 10

Radial

Slide Sorter view

Slide Sorter view is often used when adding the finishing touches to your presentation, e.g. adding special effects and summary slides. Your slides are displayed in miniature in this view.

Basic steps

1 Click the **Slide Sorter view** tool ⊞ to go into Slide Sorter View

Each slide is displayed in miniature

2 Click the **Normal View** tool 回, or use **View > Normal**, to return to Normal view

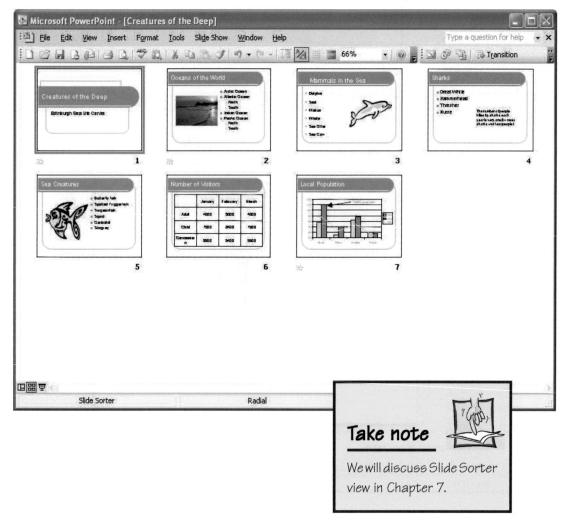

Take note

We will discuss Slide Sorter view in Chapter 7.

Basic steps

Slide Show view

1 Click the **Slide Show** tool 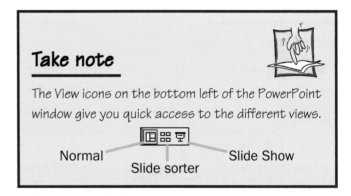 to display your slide show (it will start at the current slide – whatever slide you are viewing in Normal view, or have selected in Slide Sorter view)

Each slide fills the whole screen

2 Click the left mouse button to display the next slide

3 Press [Esc] to exit Slide Show view at any time

Your presentation will be delivered in Slide Show view. In this view, each slide takes up the full screen. When you actually deliver your presentation, it will often be projected onto a screen so that your audience can see it easily. You can go into Slide Show view at any time to see how your slide looks in this view.

Take note

The View icons on the bottom left of the PowerPoint window give you quick access to the different views.

Normal   Slide Show

Slide sorter

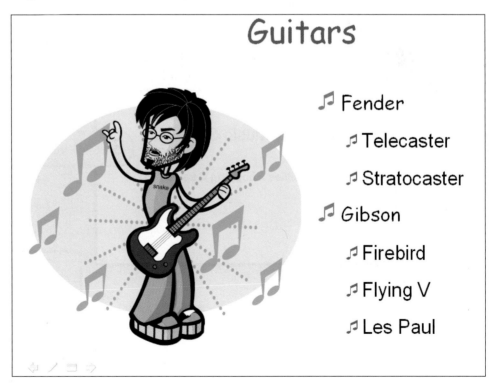

Create a presentation

When you start PowerPoint, a new blank presentation is created automatically, with a title slide layout, and the Getting Started task pane displayed on the right.

If PowerPoint is already up and running, it is easy to create a new blank presentation file.

Most presentations have a title slide as their first slide – to display the presentation subject, and perhaps the name of the presenter or the company.

The rectangular areas with a dotted outside border on a slide are called placeholders. The objects on your slides – text, clip art, graph, etc. – are positioned within a placeholder.

Basic steps

1 Click the **New** tool on the Standard toolbar

2 Click inside the Title placeholder and type in the title, 'City Music Store'

3 Click inside the Subtitle placeholder and type in the subtitle, 'St Giles Shopping Centre'

4 Click on your slide, outside the placeholders

Take note

We will add more slides to this presentation in the next chapter.

12

Basic steps

1 Open the **File** menu

2 Click **Save**

Or

3 Click the **Save** tool 💾 on the Standard toolbar

4 Specify where you want your presentation to be saved

5 Give it a relevant file name, e.g. City Music Store

6 Click [Save]

Save file

When you create a new presentation it is given a temporary file name – *Presentation1*, *Presentation2*, etc. At some stage you must save it, and give it a name that reflects its contents. You can save at any time – but it is safer to do it sooner rather than later, and save it regularly as the presentation develops.

By default, your files will be saved in the My Documents folder. To change this, and other default settings, e.g. User Name, open the **Tools** menu and select **Options**. The default folder is set on the **Save** tab, the user name on the **General** tab.

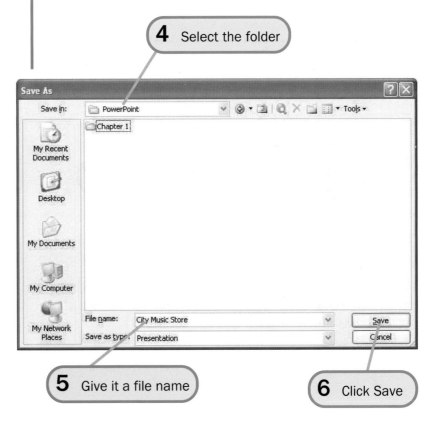

4 Select the folder

5 Give it a file name

6 Click Save

Save vs Save As

The first time you save a presentation, you are taken to the Save As dialog box where you specify the drive and/or folder that the file is to be saved in, and give it a name. Thereafter, any time you save the presentation using the Save tool , the saved file is replaced by the new, edited version. If you want to keep the original AND the edited version, you can save the edited version with a different filename or file type, or in a different location, from the Save As dialog box.

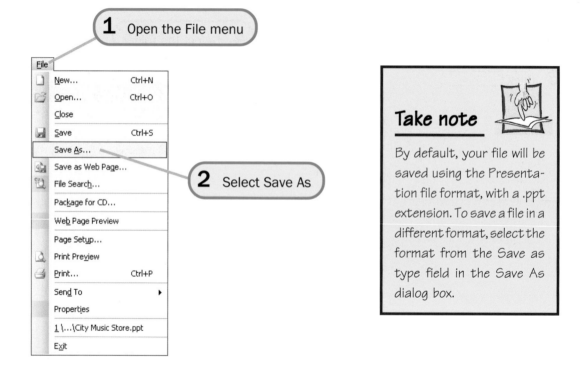

1 Open the File menu

2 Select Save As

Take note

By default, your file will be saved using the Presentation file format, with a .ppt extension. To save a file in a different format, select the format from the Save as type field in the Save As dialog box.

14

Basic steps

1 Open the **File** menu

2 Click **Open**

Or

3 Click the **Open** tool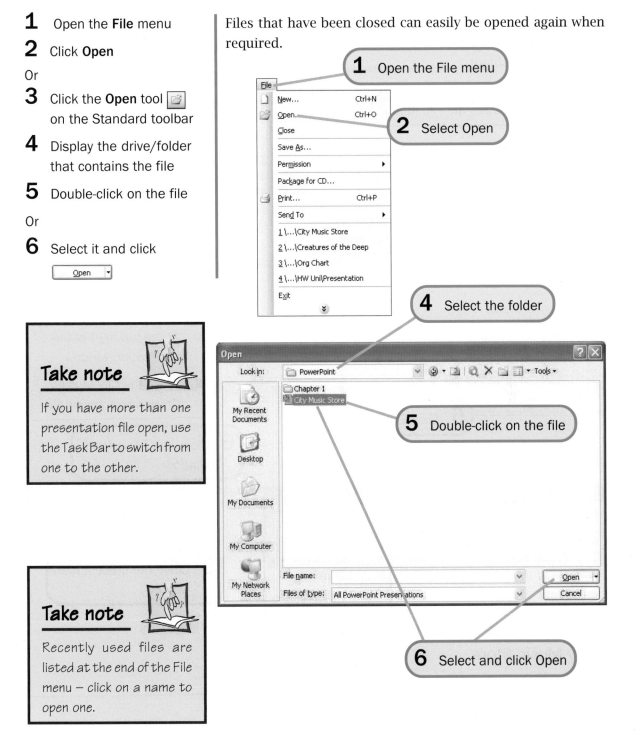
on the Standard toolbar

4 Display the drive/folder
that contains the file

5 Double-click on the file

Or

6 Select it and click

| Open | ▾ |

Files that have been closed can easily be opened again when required.

1 Open the File menu

2 Select Open

File
- New...   Ctrl+N
- Open.   Ctrl+O
- Close
- Save As...
- Permission   ▸
- Package for CD...
- Print...   Ctrl+P
- Send To   ▸
- 1 \...\City Music Store
- 2 \...\Creatures of the Deep
- 3 \...\Org Chart
- 4 \...\HW Uni\Presentation
- Exit

4 Select the folder

5 Double-click on the file

6 Select and click Open

Take note

If you have more than one presentation file open, use the Task Bar to switch from one to the other.

Take note

Recently used files are listed at the end of the File menu – click on a name to open one.

Close and Exit

When you have finished working with your file, you should save it and close it. You should also exit PowerPoint when you have finished using it.

Basic steps

- **To close a file**
1 Open the **File** menu
2 Choose **Close**

Or

3 Click the **Close** button ⌧ at the top right of the Presentation file window

- **To exit PowerPoint**
4 Open the **File** menu
5 Choose **Exit**

Or

6 Click the **Close** button ⌧ at the top right of the application window

- Close the City Music Store presentation file.

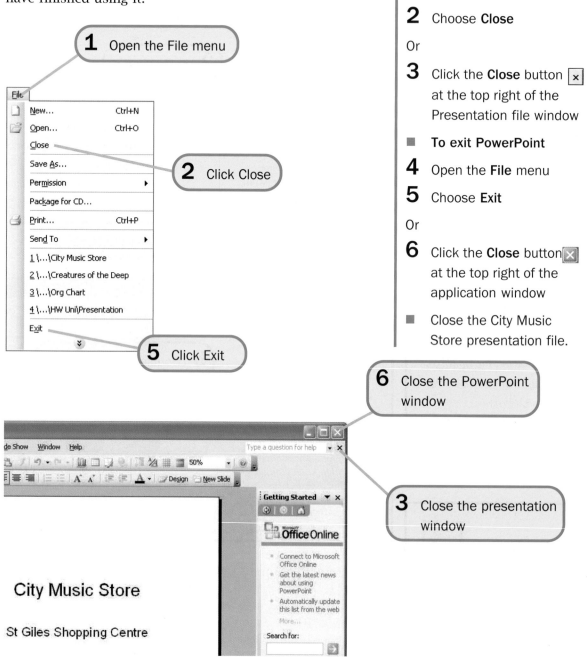

1 Open the File menu

2 Click Close

5 Click Exit

6 Close the PowerPoint window

3 Close the presentation window

City Music Store

St Giles Shopping Centre

Basic steps

- **To display the task pane**

1 Click the **Help** tool on the Standard toolbar

Or

2 Press [**F1**]

When working in PowerPoint, there is always plenty of Help available – the trick is being able to find it. There are several ways to get Help – most very intuitive and easy to use.

The Help task pane is divided into three main areas:

◆ Offline Help can be accessed from the **Search for:** field and the **Table of Contents** option in the top of the pane.

◆ Online Help can be accessed from the middle area.

◆ Specific areas covering topics like 'What's New', 'Contact Us' and 'Accessibility Help' can be accessed from the **See also** list at the bottom of the task pane.

Take note

The Back and Forward icons at the top of a pane take you backwards and forwards through the panes that you have used recently. The Home icon takes you to the Getting Started task pane that is displayed when you open the application.

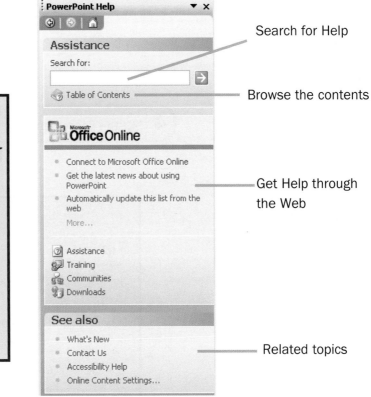

Search for Help

Browse the contents

Get Help through the Web

Related topics

Search for Help

You can search for Help system using the **Type a question for help** box on the Menu bar, or the **Search for** field in the Help task pane.

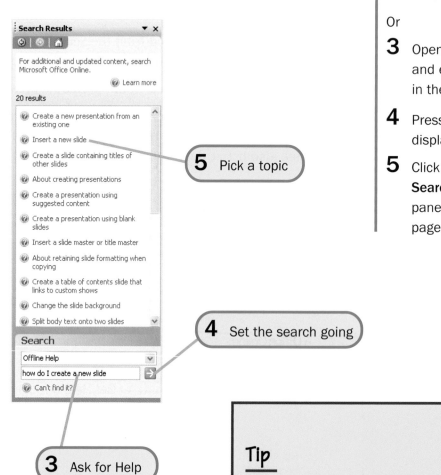

Basic steps

1 Type in your question

> how do I create a new slide ▾

2 Press [**Enter**]

Or

3 Open the **Help** task pane and enter the keyword(s) in the **Search for:** field

4 Press [**Enter**] or → to display a list of topics

5 Click on a topic in the **Search Results** task pane to display the Help page

Tip

If you can't find the Help that you need, click Can't find it? at the bottom of the Search Results task pane – PowerPoint will give you suggestions on how you could make your search more successful.

You can also search another location in the Search options at the bottom of the Search Results task pane, or try searching for different keywords.

Basic steps

1 Click the **Table of Contents** 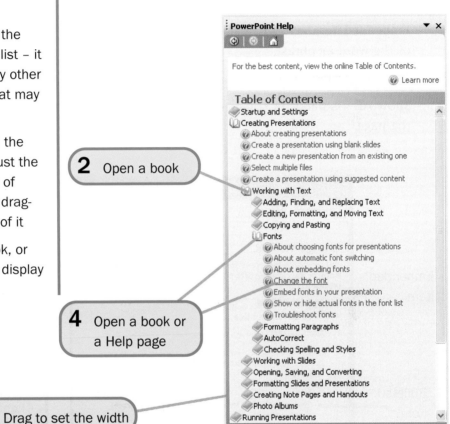 option near the top of the Help task pane

2 Click on a book in the Table of Contents list – it will open to display other books or topics that may interest you

3 If you cannot read the entries in full, adjust the width of the Table of Contents pane by dragging the left edge of it

4 Open another book, or click on a topic to display its Help page

Table of Contents

You can browse through the Help available using the Table of Contents option.

2 Open a book

4 Open a book or a Help page

3 Drag to set the width

Hot spots

On a Help page, some text may be blue. This indicates a 'hot spot' that can display some information. The most common types of hot spots are:

◆ **Bulleted item** - displays a list of instructions

◆ **Embedded item** – gives (usually in green) an explanation of the word or phrase

◆ **Tip** - suggested Help

◆ **Show All** - expands or collapses all of the hot spots on the page.

Help page tools

☐ Tiles the windows and the Help page panel

☐ Untiles the windows and the Help page panel

⇦ Takes you back through the Help pages viewed

⇨ Takes you forward through the Help pages viewed

🖨 Prints the Help page

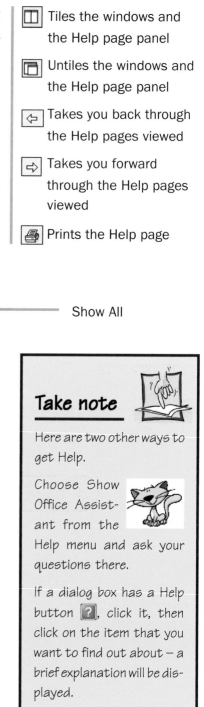

Embedded item

Bulleted item

Tip

Show All

Take note

Here are two other ways to get Help.

Choose Show Office Assistant from the Help menu and ask your questions there.

If a dialog box has a Help button **?**, click it, then click on the item that you want to find out about – a brief explanation will be displayed.

On-line Help

1 Open the **Help** menu and choose **Microsoft Office Online**

Or

2 Access the on-line Help from the middle area of the Help task pane

3 Navigate your way through the Help pages until you find the information required

If you cannot find the Help that you need in the normal Help system, visit the Microsoft Office Online site for updated Help files, answers to top support issues and frequently asked questions on PowerPoint, tips and templates.

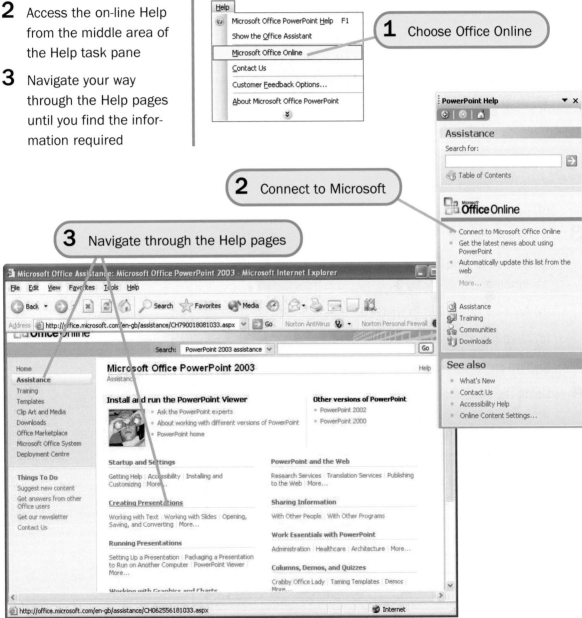

Exercises

1 Complete the following sentence, by filling in the gaps, using the words:

file   outline   presentation   notes pages

PowerPoint is a _____ graphics package. Each _____ may contain slides, handouts, _____ and an _____.

2 A slide can be used to display a selection of different objects. Give four examples of the types of objects that you may display on a slide.

(a) ....

(b) ....

(c) ....

(d) ....

3 A placeholder is:

(a) Someone who keeps your place in a queue for the cinema

(b) An area on a slide in which an object is placed

(c) A setting at a dinner table

(d) The panel displayed down the left side of the screen.

4 Using the Help if necessary, give the keyboard shortcuts that would carry out the same function as the tools displayed in the table:

Tool	Purpose	Keyboard shortcut
🗋	Create a new presentation file	
📂	Open an existing file	
💾	Save a file	
✖	Close the application	

5   In Normal view, suggest two ways in which the Outline/ Slides pane and notes pane can be displayed if they have been closed.

(a) ....

(b) ....

6   Label the View icons appropriately

7   Suggest three ways of moving from slide to slide in Normal view.

(a) ....

(b) ....

(c) ....

8   To display the Microsoft Office PowerPoint Help panel you would click:

(a)   (b)   (c)   (d)

9   Display the Table of Contents, and open the Startup and Settings book. Go to the section on Creating Presentations. Read the topic 'About creating Presentations'.

10   Using the **Type a question for help** box, locate information on bullet points.

Read the section on 'Move text in an outline'. List three methods you can use to move text and adjust the structure of your slide.

(a) ....

(b) ....

(c) ....

11 Use the Office Assistant to find out how to insert a new slide. What are the two methods suggested?

(a) ....

(b) ....

12 Which function key displays the PowerPoint Help panel?

13 Locate Help on changing the slide background colour using the Help panel. Read the information that you find.

14 If you have Internet access, go to training on Microsoft Office Online and explore any topic that interests you.

2 Text

Adding a new slide

New slides can be inserted at any position in a presentation file. A bulleted list layout is normally used to display text and is the default slide layout. We will discuss the various layouts as we progress through the book.

◆ Open the City Music Store presentation file.

Take note

To delete a slide, select it in the Outline/ Slides pane and press [Delete] or open the Edit menu and select Delete Slide.

1 In Normal view, display the slide that will be before your new one – click on it in the Outline/ Slides pane

2 Click the **New Slide** tool or press **[Enter]** – a new bulleted list slide, will be inserted and the **Slide Layout** task pane will appear

3 To change the layout of the slide, scroll through the layouts and select the one required

4 If you have changed the slide layout, apply the single bulleted list layout to the slide again

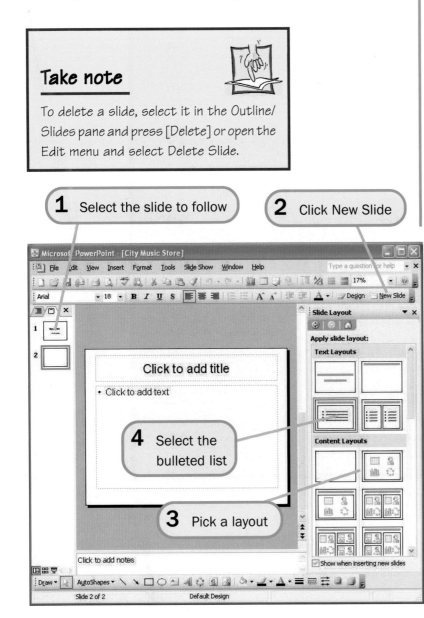

1 Select the slide to follow

2 Click New Slide

4 Select the bulleted list

3 Pick a layout

Tip

If the Slide Layout task pane does not appear, the ☑ Show when inserting new slides checkbox at the bottom of the pane will have been deselected. To display the pane, choose Task Pane from the View menu.

Bulleted lists

1 Click inside the Title placeholder and type in your title, 'Student Instruments' in this case

2 Click inside the bulleted list placeholder and type the items, pressing [Enter] after each one – use in the following list:

    Woodwind

    Clarinet

    Oboe

    Saxophone

    Brass

    Trumpet

    Trombone

3 Click on your slide, outside the placeholders

We have already added text to the Title slide in the City Music Store presentation. Adding and editing text to the bulleted list slide layout is just as easy.

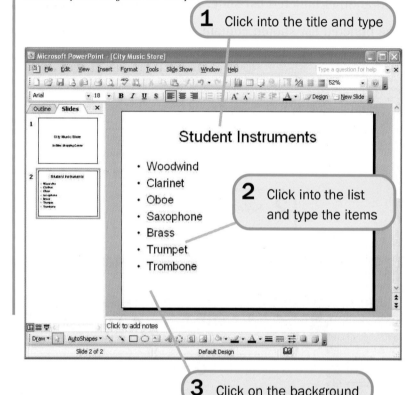

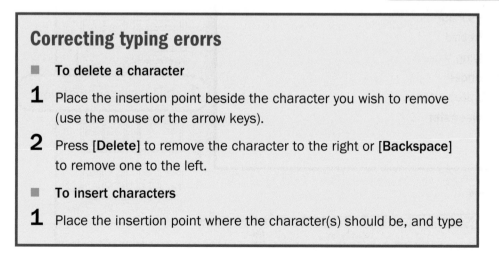

Correcting typing erorrs

▪ **To delete a character**

1 Place the insertion point beside the character you wish to remove (use the mouse or the arrow keys).

2 Press [**Delete**] to remove the character to the right or [**Backspace**] to remove one to the left.

▪ **To insert characters**

1 Place the insertion point where the character(s) should be, and type

Add a slide

Explore the alternative ways of adding new slides while adding this one to your file.

Add another bulleted list slide. The title should be 'Guitars'.

The bulleted list should contain:

    Gibson
    Les Paul
    Firebird
    Flying V
    Fender
    Stratocaster
    Telecaster

2 Select Insert New Slide from the list

Basic steps

1 Right-click on the slide layout in the **Slide Layout** task pane

Or

2 Click the down arrow to the right of the layout and select **Insert New Slide** from the options

Or

3 Use the keyboard shortcut **[Ctrl]-[M]**

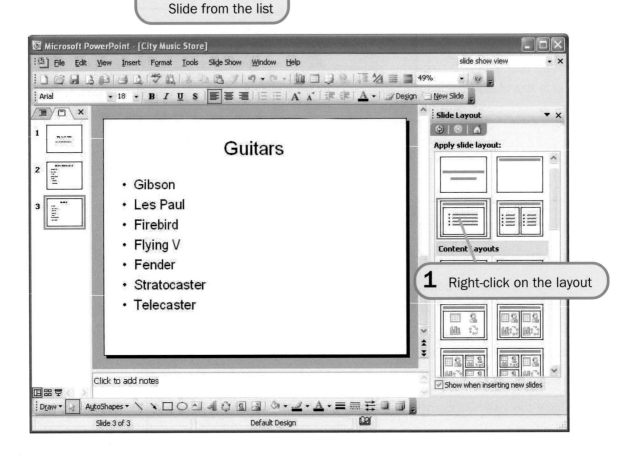

1 Right-click on the layout

Adjusting the indent

1 Click anywhere in the Clarinet bullet point

2 Click 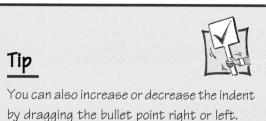 the **Increase Indent** tool

3 Repeat for Oboe, Saxophone, Trumpet and Trombone – to indent several adjacent bullet points at once, select them and click

4 On the Guitars slide, indent the Les Paul, Firebird and Flying V under Gibson, and indent the Stratocaster and Telecaster under Fender

The bullet points on your slides will be structured – you will have main points (at the first bulleted level) and some of these points will have sub-points (at the second, third, fourth or even fifth level).

Initially, all bullet points on your slide are at level 1. You can easily increase or decrease the indent of bullet points to create the structure required.

◆ Display the Student Instrument slide in the City Music Store presentation file.

Tip

You can also increase or decrease the indent by dragging the bullet point right or left.

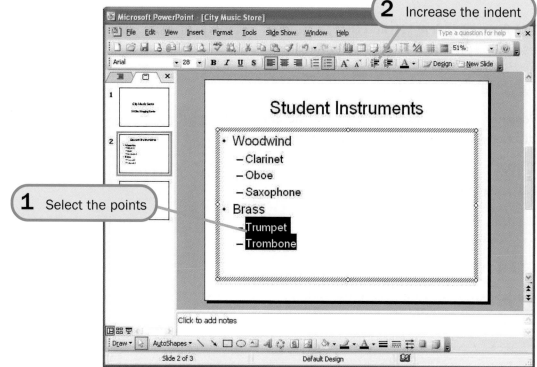

29

Indent levels

You can increase the indent on bullet points to create a structure up to 5 levels deep.

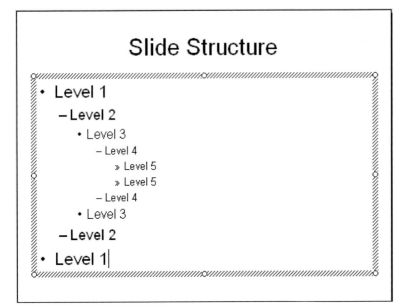

The Increase Indent and Decrease Indent tools can be used to create the structure required.

Keyboard shortcuts

Position the insertion in front of the point you wish to increase/decrease the indent of and press:

[Tab]   to increase the indent

[Shift]-[Tab]   to decrease the indent.

Position the insertion point anywhere within the point you wish to increase/decrease the indent of and press:

[Shift]-[Alt]-[→]   to increase the indent

[Shift]-[Alt]-[←]   to decrease the indent.

Basic steps

1 To undo an action, click **Undo**  on the Stand-ard toolbar

2 To undo several actions at once, click the down arrow on the **Undo**tool and highlight down to the earliest action to undo

3 To redo the last action that you undid, click **Redo**

4 To redo several actions, drop down the **Redo** list and highlight down to the earliest action

Take note

You cannot undo (or redo) selected actions back up the list—you can only undo/ redo a sequence of actions working backwards from the latest.

Undo and Redo

There are different types of actions that you can undo: adding/deleting slides, applying formatting, editing text, etc. You can also undo actions that PowerPoint makes automatically using the AutoCorrect feature, e.g. capitalising the first letter of a sentence.

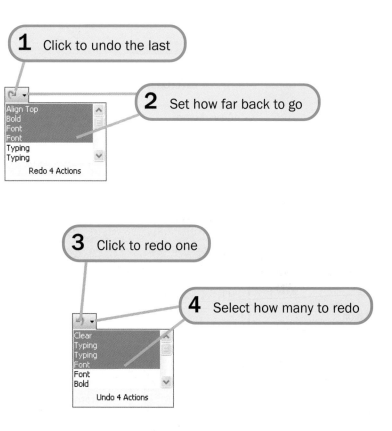

Moving text

The bullet points on your slides can be moved using cut and paste or drag and drop techniques.

Basic steps

- **Cut and Paste**

1 Select the bullet point – click on it (its substructure will automatically be selected too)

2 Click the **Cut** tool

3 Position the insertion point where you want to move the point to

4 Click the **Paste** tool

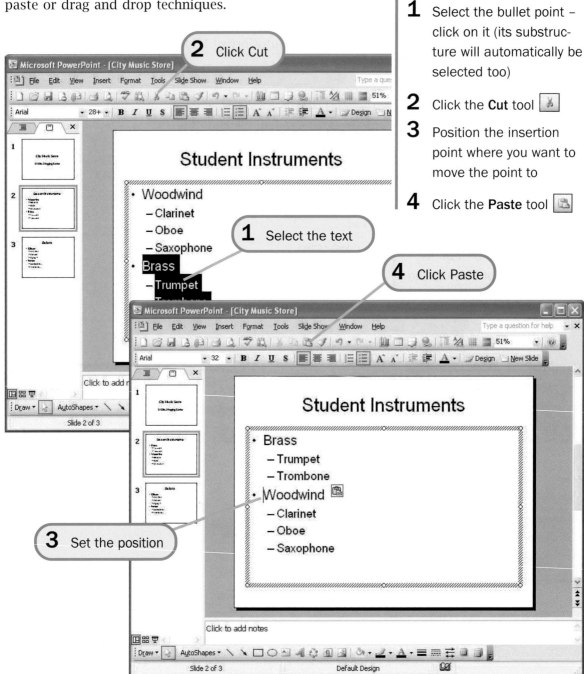

2 Click Cut

1 Select the text

4 Click Paste

3 Set the position

Basic steps

■ **Drag and Drop**

1 Select the bullet point

2 Drag the bullet point to the its position – the horizontal line will show you where you are

3 Let go of the mouse button

Keyboard shortcuts

Cut **[Ctrl]-[X]**   Cut **[Ctrl]-[C]**   Paste **[Ctrl]-[V]**

Click anywhere in the point you wish to move and:

[Shift]-[Alt]-[↑]   to move it up

[Shift]-[Alt]-[↓]   to move down

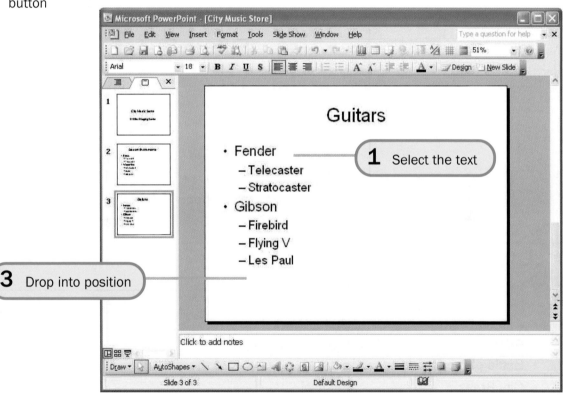

◆ Rearrange the instruments on the Student Instruments slide into descending alphabetical order using either technique.

◆ Rearrange the guitars slide, so that the Fenders are before the Gibsons, and the models within each group are in ascending order.

Add and arrange a slide

Add one more slide to the City Music Store presentation file.

Use the double bulleted list layout, and complete the Future Events information as displayed.

Rearrange the bullet points into ascending alphabetical order.

◆ You can drag and drop the items in each column if your wish, but you will need to use cut and paste to move items from one column to the other.

Moving/copying slides

- **To move a slide**

1 Select the slide on the Outline/Slides tab

2 Click the **Cut** tool

3 In the Outline/Slides tab, click where the slide is to go

4 Click the **Paste** tool

- **To copy a slide**

5 Select the slide

6 Click the **Copy** tool

7 In the Outline/Slides tab, click where you want the copy to appear

8 Click the **Paste** tool

You can easily move or copy slides within and between presentation files.

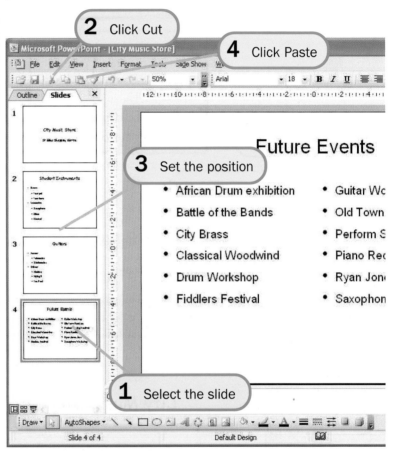

Take note

Drag and drop can be used to move slides within a file. Select the slide in the Outline/Slides tab, and drag and drop it into the required position. To copy the slide, hold down [Ctrl] as you drag and drop.

Moving and copying between files

You can easily move and copy slides between files using Cut, Copy and Paste.

Tip

You can also copy and move slides in Slide Sorter view.

Basic steps

1. Open the files that you wish to copy to and from
2. In the source file select the slide to move or copy
3. Click the **Cut** or **Copy** tool
4. Switch to the target file
5. On the Outline/Slides tab, click where you want the slide to appear
6. Click the **Paste** tool

1 Select the slide

2 Click Cut/Copy

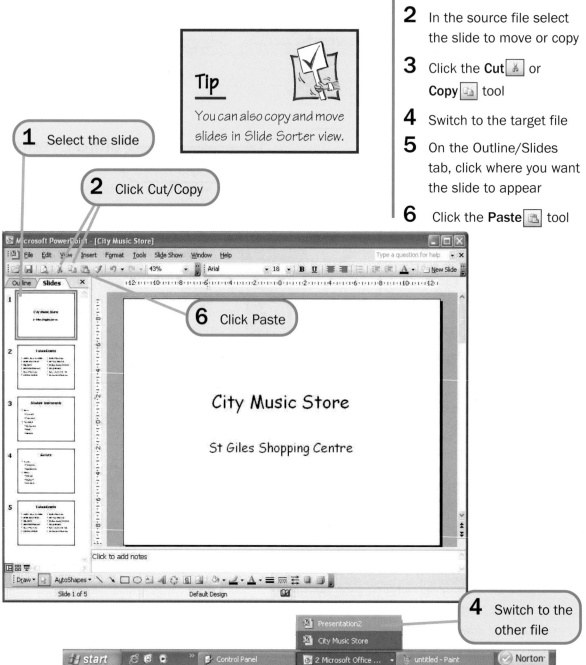

6 Click Paste

City Music Store

St Giles Shopping Centre

4 Switch to the other file

Font formatting

1 Select the text you want to format

2 Choose a font from the Font list

3 Pick the font size you want from the Size list

4 Click the Bold, Italic, Underline or Shadow tools to switch the format on or off

5 Select a colour from the Font colour options

6 Deselect the text

Text can be formatted using the Formatting toolbar or the Format menu.

Tip

To change the size of selected text, click A⁺ to increase or A⁻ to decrease it to the next size in the Font Size list.

3 Set the size

4 Add/remove emphasis

5 Set the colour

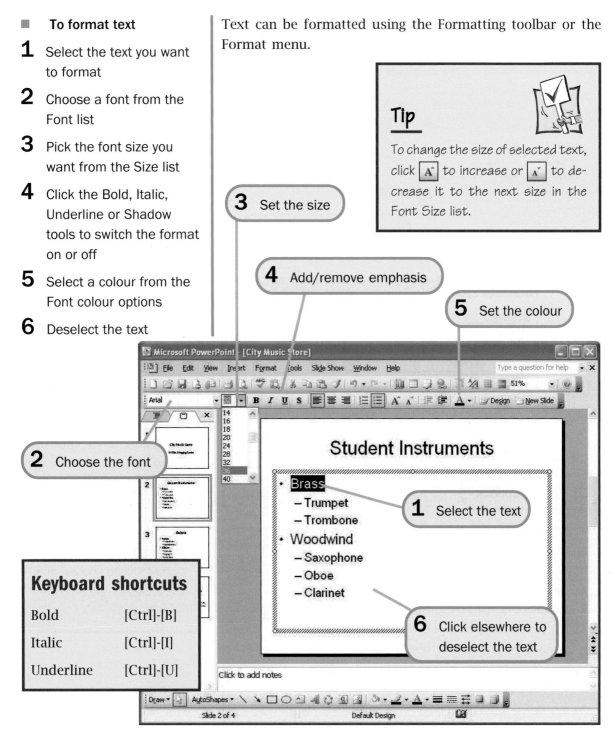

2 Choose the font

1 Select the text

6 Click elsewhere to deselect the text

Keyboard shortcuts

Bold	[Ctrl]-[B]
Italic	[Ctrl]-[I]
Underline	[Ctrl]-[U]

The Font dialog box

You can also go to the Font dialog box to format the text on your slide.

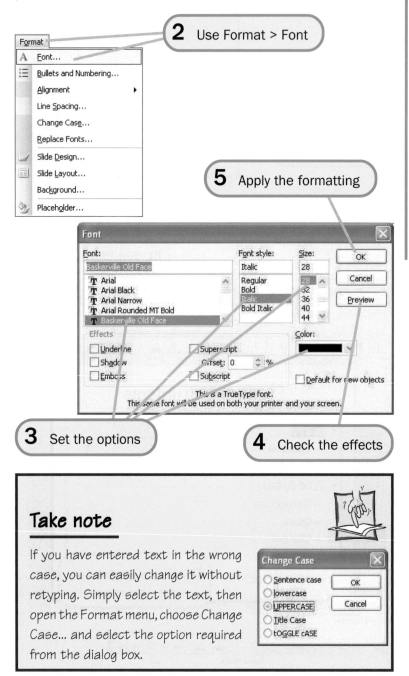

Basic steps

1 Select the text to format

2 Choose **Font...** from the **Format** menu

3 Set your format options

4 Click ⟨ Preview ⟩ to see how your selections look (you may have to move the Font dialog box aside)

5 Click ⟨ OK ⟩ if you want to apply the formats

Or

6 Click ⟨ Cancel ⟩ to leave things as they were

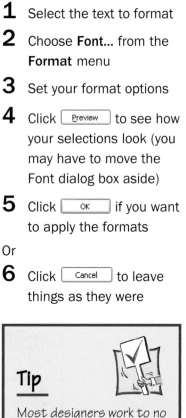

Tip

Most designers work to no more than three different fonts per page/slide, using different sizes, bold and italic for extra variety.

Don't change the formatting on every slide. If you overdo things you will give the presentation an inconsistent look.

Take note

If you have entered text in the wrong case, you can easily change it without retyping. Simply select the text, then open the Format menu, choose Change Case... and select the option required from the dialog box.

Change Case

- ○ Sentence case
- ○ lowercase
- ● UPPERCASE
- ○ Title Case
- ○ tOGGLE cASE

OK   Cancel

Paragraph formatting

1 Select the text you want to format

2 Click on the **Left** ≣, **Centre** ≣ or **Right Alignment** ≣ tool

3 If you have selected multiple paragraphs or several characters, deselect the text

Alignment

In presentation files, text is usually aligned to the left or centre of the placeholder. There are tools for both of these and for right alignment on the Formatting toolbar. If you want text to be justified (making the text meet both left and right margins), there is an option on the Format > Alignment menu.

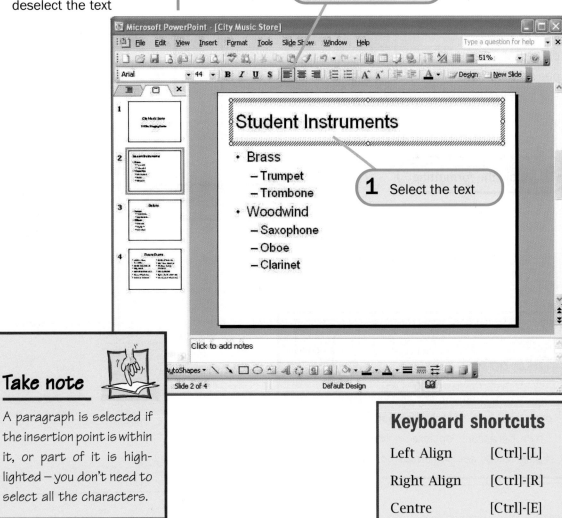

Take note

A paragraph is selected if the insertion point is within it, or part of it is highlighted – you don't need to select all the characters.

Keyboard shortcuts

Left Align	[Ctrl]-[L]
Right Align	[Ctrl]-[R]
Centre	[Ctrl]-[E]

Line Spacing

The default line spacing is single. The line spacing between the paragraphs can be adjusted from the Line Spacing dialog box. You could use this option if you have only a few bullet points on a slide and you want to distribute them more evenly within the placeholder.

Basic steps

1 Select the paragraphs you want to adjust the line spacing for

2 Open the **Format** menu and choose **Line Spacing**

3 Specify the line spacing options required

4 Click [Preview] to see the effect of your selections (you may have to move the dialog box aside)

5 Click [OK] if you want to apply the new settings

Or

6 Click [Cancel] to leave things as they were

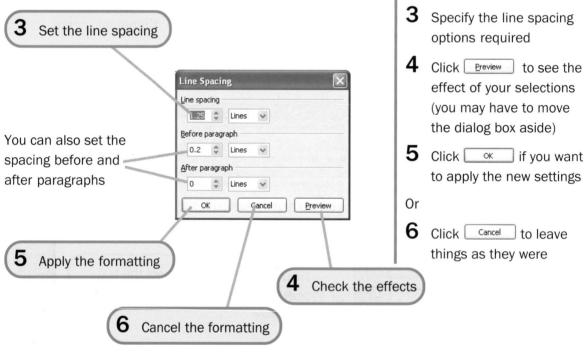

3 Set the line spacing

You can also set the spacing before and after paragraphs

5 Apply the formatting

6 Cancel the formatting

4 Check the effects

Take note

You can also adjust the spacing between your paragraphs by setting the Before paragraph/ After paragraph options in the Line Spacing dialog box to get the effect you require.

40

Formatting bullets

1 Select the point(s)

2 Open the **Format** menu and choose **Bullets and Numbering...**

3 Go to the **Bulleted** tab

4 Select a bullet

5 Set the colour and size

6 Click [OK]

In most slide layouts the text objects are formatted to display bullets at each point. The bullets can be switched off (and on again) by clicking [≣].

You can also select an alternative bullet point from the huge range available.

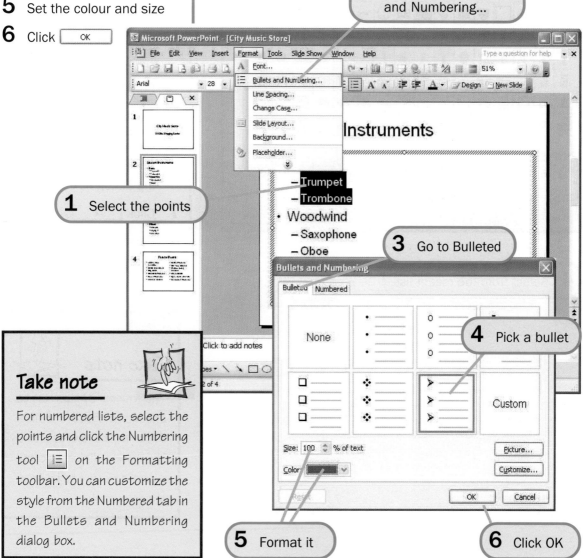

2 Use Format > Bullets and Numbering...

1 Select the points

3 Go to Bulleted

4 Pick a bullet

5 Format it

6 Click OK

Take note

For numbered lists, select the points and click the Numbering tool [≣] on the Formatting toolbar. You can customize the style from the Numbered tab in the Bullets and Numbering dialog box.

Customized bullets

You can select from an even greater choice of bullets by going into the Symbol dialog box.

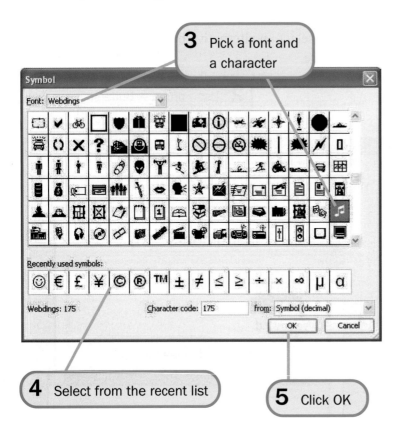

3 Pick a font and a character

4 Select from the recent list

5 Click OK

Basic steps

1 Work through steps 1–3 on the previous page

2 Click [Customize...]

3 At the Symbol dialog box, select a character set in the Font: field and choose a character

Or

4 Select a character from the **Recently used symbols:** row

5 Click [OK]

6 Set the colour and size at the Bullets and Numbering dialog box

7 Click [OK]

■ Close the City Music Store presentation file

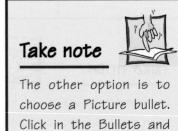

Take note

The other option is to choose a Picture bullet. Click in the Bullets and Numbering dialog box and select a picture bullet from those available.

Westside Sports

Activities for Everyone

Children's Classes

- Swimming
- Tennis
- Badminton
- Judo
- Gymnastics

Activities on Offer

- Fencing
- Karate
- Squash
- Badminton
- Swimming
- Diving
- Judo
- Tennis
- Gymnastics
- Table Tennis
- Volleyball
- Basketball

A: Westside Sports

1 Create a new blank presentation, with a Title Slide layout for the first slide.

2 Enter the title, 'Westside Sports' and the subtitle, 'Activities for Everyone'.

3 Add a new slide to your presentation, with a single bulleted list layout.

4 The slide title should be 'Children's Classes'.

5 The bullet points should read:

- Swimming
- Tennis
- Badminton
- Judo
- Gymnastics

6 Add another new slide, with a double bulleted list layout

7 The slide title should be 'Activities on offer'

8 The bullets in the left and right sides should read:

- Fencing
- Karate
- Squash
- Badminton
- Swimming
- Diving
- Judo
- Tennis
- Gymnastics
- Table Tennis
- Volleyball
- Basketball

9 Save your presentation file – call it 'Westside Sports'.

10 Add a slide with a bulleted list layout at the end of the file.

11 Enter 'Certificated Courses' in the title.

12 List the items: 'National Pool Lifeguard', 'Fitness Instructor', 'Health related exercise for children' and 'Aqua Fit Instructor'.

13 Move slide 3 above slide 2.

14 Save the edited file as 'Westside Sports *your initials*'.

Close your presentation file

B: Creatures of the Deep

1 Create a new blank presentation, with a Title Slide layout for the first slide.

2 Enter the title, ' Creatures of the Deep' and the subtitle, 'Edinburgh Sea Life Centre'.

3 Add a new slide, with a single bulleted list layout.

4 The slide title should be 'Oceans of the World'.

5 The bullet points should read:

- Arctic Ocean
- Atlantic Ocean
- North
- South
- Indian Ocean
- Pacific Ocean

6 Add another new slide, with a double bulleted list layout.

7 The slide title should be 'Mammals in the Sea'.

8 The bullets in the left and right sides should read:

• Orca	• Sea Lion
• Dolphin	• Walrus
• Elephant Seal	• Grey Whale
• Grey Seal	• Humpback Whale
• Sea Cow	• Sea Otter
• Porpoise	• Minke Whale

9 Save your presentation file – call it 'Creatures of the Deep'.

Creatures of the Deep

Edinburgh Sea Life Centre

Oceans of the World

- Arctic Ocean
- Atlantic Ocean
  - North
  - South
- Indian Ocean
- Pacific Ocean

Mammals in the Sea

• Orca	• Sea Lion
• Dolphin	• Walrus
• Elephant Seal	• Grey Whale
• Grey Seal	• Humpback Whale
• Sea Cow	• Sea Otter
• Porpoise	• Minke Whale

10 Add a slide with a bulleted list layout at the end of the file.

11 Enter 'Press Releases' in the title.

12 List 'New Dolphin Research', 'Upgrade to Babies Pool', 'Outreach Initiative' and 'New Rescue Hotline' on the slide.

13 Copy slide 2 and paste it below slide 3.

14 Save the edited version of the file as 'Creatures of the Deep *your initials*'.

Close your presentation file.

C: Westside Sports, formatting

1 Open the presentation file Westside Sports.

2 On the title slide, change the size of the title to 60, and the subtitle to 44.

3 Format the title to have a shadow effect and the subtitle to be in italics.

4 On slide 2, Children's Classes, rearrange the bullet points into ascending alphabetical order.

5 Set the line spacing for the items to 1.5.

6 Change the font on this slide to Comic Sans MS.

7 The slide title should be red.

8 Bulleted items 1, 3 and 5 should be blue.

9 Bulleted items 2 and 4 should be green.

10 On slide 3, Activities on Offer, rearrange the bullet points into ascending alphabetical order, keeping six items in each bulleted list.

11 Set the line spacing in each list to 1.5.

12 Save your file.

Close the Westside Sports presentation file

Westside Sports

Activities for Everyone

Children's Classes

- Badminton
- Gymnastics
- Judo
- Swimming
- Tennis

Activities on Offer

- Badminton
- Basketball
- Diving
- Fencing
- Gymnastics
- Judo
- Karate
- Squash
- Swimming
- Table Tennis
- Tennis
- Volleyball

B: Creatures of the Deep, formatting

1   Open your presentation 'Creatures of the Deep'.

2   On the title slide, change the size of the title to 54, and the subtitle to 40.

3   Format the title to be bold and in italics and add a shadow effect to the subtitle.

4   On slide 2, Oceans of the World, rearrange the bullet points into descending alphabetical order.

5   Set the line spacing for the items to 1.3.

6   On slide 3, Mammals in the Sea, add a new bullet point, 'Seal' and put 'Elephant' and 'Grey' as sub-points under it (remove 'seal' from these entries).

7   Add a bullet point, 'Whale' and put 'Grey', 'Humpback', 'Minke' and 'Orca' under it (remove 'whale' from these).

8   Rearrange the main points into ascending alphabetical order.

9   Rearrange the sub-points into ascending alphabetical order.

10   Set the line spacing for the left side list to have 0 spacing before and 1.0 after each paragraph.

11   Change the level 1 bullet points on slide 2 and 3 to a ✓.

12   Save your file.

Close the Creatures of the Deep presentation file.

Creatures of the Deep

Edinburgh Sea Life Centre

Oceans of the World

✓ Pacific Ocean
✓ Indian Ocean
✓ Atlantic Ocean
   – South
   – North
✓ Arctic Ocean

Mammals in the Sea

✓ Dolphin	✓ Seal
	– Elephant
✓ Porpoise	– Grey
	✓ Walrus
✓ Sea Cow	✓ Whale
	– Grey
✓ Sea Lion	– Humpback
	– Minke
✓ Sea Otter	– Orca

3 Layout and design

Change slide layout

So far, we have created new slides with bulleted lists on them – either a single or a double list of bullet points. We have also seen that there are many other slide layouts to choose from.

You will normally specify the slide layout you want when you create a slide. However, you can also change the slide layout of an existing slide if you wish.

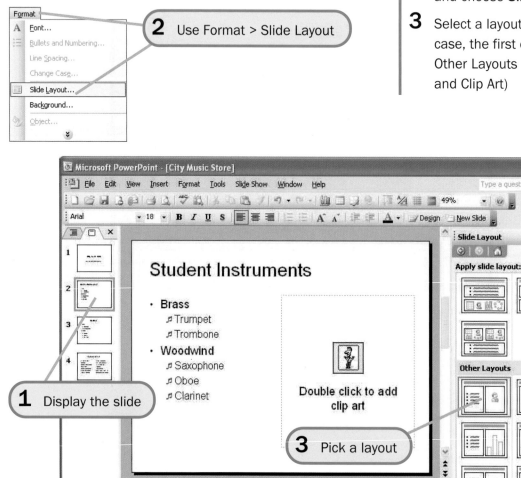

2 Use Format > Slide Layout

1 Display the slide

3 Pick a layout

Basic steps

1 Open the **Format** menu and choose **Background**

2 Select a background colour from the list

Or

3 Click **More Colors...** and/ or **Fill Effects...** and select from the dialog boxes

4 Click [Preview] to see the effect on your slide

Or

5 Click [Apply] to apply it to the selected slide

6 Click [Apply to All] to apply to all slides

7 Click [Cancel] if you don't like the effect

In the previous chapter we considered the options available for formatting text. You can also add interest by formatting the background of the slides, adding a colour or special effect.

If a presentation is in sections e.g. on individual departments, or regional figures, you can set a different background colour for each section.

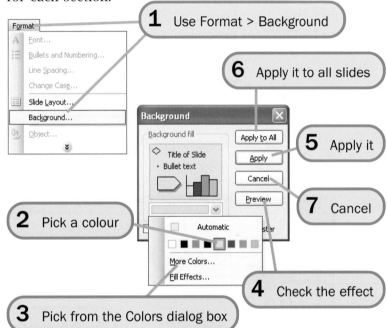

1 Use Format > Background

6 Apply it to all slides

5 Apply it

7 Cancel

2 Pick a colour

4 Check the effect

3 Pick from the Colors dialog box

Tip

You can select more than one slide at once using the slides tab. To select:

Adjacent slides — Click on the first, hold **[Shift]** down and click on the last one you want

Non-adjacent slides — Hold **[Ctrl]** down and click on each slide you want

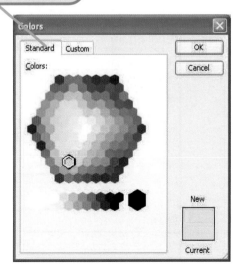

Slide design templates

The files that we have created so far have all used the Default design template. This is a blank slide – with a white slide background, Arial black font, round bullets, etc.

There are also a number of professionally designed templates that you can choose from. The template determines the design elements of your presentation – colour, fonts, alignment of text, bullet style, etc. They can give a very polished and consistent look to your presentation – well worth exploring!

2 Use Format > Slide Design

3 Pick a design

City Music Store

St Giles Shopping Centre

4 Go online for more

1 Double-click the name

Basic steps

1 Open the **View** menu and choose **Header and Footer...**

2 Select the appropriate tab - **Slide** or **Notes and Handouts**

3 Tick the items you want to appear, giving details as needed

4 Click [Apply] to add a header or footer to the selected slides only,

Or

5 [Apply to All] to add to all slides

Headers and Footers are used to add slide numbers, the date, time or any other standard text to the top or bottom of slides, notes or handouts.

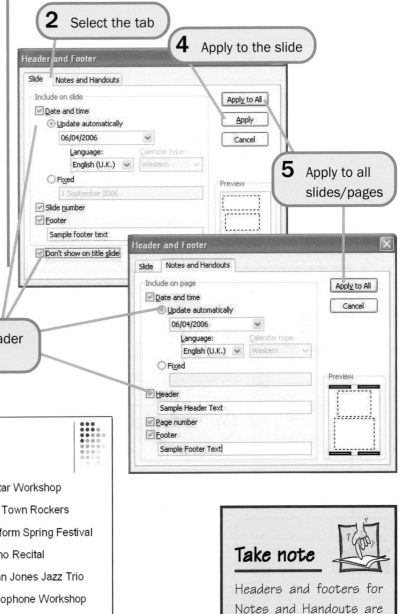

2 Select the tab

4 Apply to the slide

5 Apply to all slides/pages

3 Define the header and footer

Future Events

- African Drum exhibition
- Battle of the Bands
- City Brass
- Classical Woodwind
- Drum Workshop
- Fiddlers Festival
- Guitar Workshop
- Old Town Rockers
- Perform Spring Festival
- Piano Recital
- Ryan Jones Jazz Trio
- Saxophone Workshop

06/04/2006   Sample footer text   4

Take note

Headers and footers for Notes and Handouts are displayed on all pages.

Masters

In the previous chapter we made changes to the text and bullet points on individual slides. If you want to change the layout in every slide in a presentation, you should make the changes to the Slide Master. This holds the formatted placeholders for the slide title and text. Any background objects you want to appear on every slide (like your company name or logo) should also be added to the Slide Master.

◆ Any slides where you have changed the text formatting at slide level will be treated as exceptions and will retain the custom formatting you applied to them.

◆ The title slide has its own master. Changes made to the Slide Master will not be reflected on your Title slide.

Basic steps

1 Open the **View** menu, choose **Master** then select **Slide Master**

Or

2 Hold down [**Shift**] and click the **Normal View** icon to go into the Slide Master, or to the Title Master if you are on the title slide at the time

3 Amend the Slide Master, using the normal formatting techniques

4 Click the **Close Master View** tool to end

The slide-title master pair

3 Format as normal

2 [Shift]-click to start

4 Close the Master view

Click to edit Master title style

Click to edit Master subtitle style

Basic steps

- **To delete a placeholder**

1 Select the placeholder and press **[Delete]**

- **To restore placeholders**

2 Click the **Master Layout** tool

3 Select the placeholders required

4 Click OK

The placeholders

The placeholders for Object Areas for AutoLayouts, Date Area, Footer Area or Number Area are all optional. They can easily be deleted – and put back again.

You can delete any of the master placeholders – if you don't want to use them.

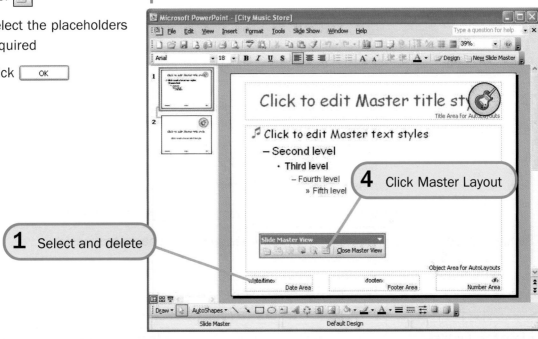

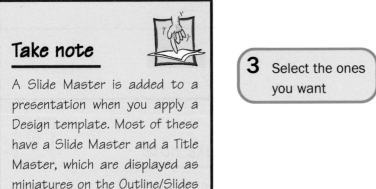

Take note

A Slide Master is added to a presentation when you apply a Design template. Most of these have a Slide Master and a Title Master, which are displayed as miniatures on the Outline/Slides tab in Master view.

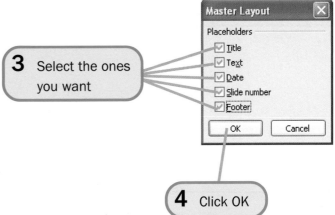

Slide Master view toolbar

| Slide Master View | ▼ |
| 🗋 ⬚ 🗐 🗐 🗐 🧾 | Close Master View |

Insert New Slide Master	Adds a new Slide Master to your presentation – each presentation must have at least one Slide Master
Insert New Title Master	Adds a new Title Master to your presentation
Delete Master	Deletes the selected master
Preserve Master	When you preserve a master you protect if from being deleted automatically by PowerPoint. When all the slides that follow a master are deleted, or another design template is applied to the slides that follow a master, PowerPoint usually deletes the slide master. If you don't want this to happen, you can preserve a master. Click the preserve Master tool to toggle the preserve status on/off.
Rename Master	Opens a dialog box where you can rename the master
Master Layout	Displays the Master Layout dialog box, where you can switch on any placeholders that you have deleted from the master
Close Master View	Returns you to the view you were in before accessing the masters

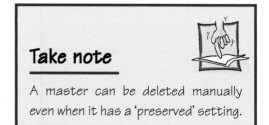

Take note

A master can be deleted manually even when it has a 'preserved' setting.

Exercises

A: City Music Store

1 Open the City Music Store file.

2 Change the slide layout of the Student Instrument slide to one with bullet points on the left and a clip art placeholder on the right.

3 Change the slide Layout on the Guitars slide to one with bullet points on the right and clip art on the left.

4 Set the background colour for the Title Slide only to a colour of your choice.

5 Go into Master Slide view.

6 If there is no Title Master, add a new one – click 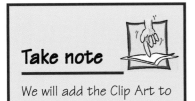.

7 Format the fonts on the Title Master to be Comic Sans MS, blue for the Title and red for the subtitle.

8 Format the font on the Slide Master to be Comic Sans MS and blue for the title.

9 Change the bullets in the first level bullet points to Webdings musical notes, or another symbol of your choice.

10 Return to Normal view and look at the effect you have created on the different slides.

11 Save and close the file.

Take note

We will add the Clip Art to these slides later.

B: Westside Sport

1 Open the Westside Sports file.

2 Change the slide layout of the Children's Classes slide to one with bullet points on the left and clip art on the right.

3 Set the background colour for all slides have a two-colour fill effect, with the shading from a corner – use pale colours so that you can still read the text clearly.

4 Go into Master Slide view.

5 Format the first level bullet point to be a symbol of your choice. Make the bullet point red, and increase the size of it if necessary (many symbols need to be enlarged to make the detail on them clear).

6 Return to Normal view and look at the effect you have created on the different slides.

7 Display slide numbers and your name in the footer of all slides except the title slide.

8 Save and close the file.

C: Creatures of the Deep

1 Open the Creatures of the Deep file.

2 Change the slide layout of the Oceans of the World slide to one with bullet points on the right and a clip art placeholder on the left.

3 Apply the Ocean design template to the presentation (or other design template of your choice).

4 Place slide numbers and today's date (fixed) on all slides except the title slide.

5 Save and close the file.

4 Graphics

Insert clip art

PowerPoint comes with hundreds of clip art pictures that can be added to your slides. In addition to the clips that come with PowerPoint, you'll find many more online.

You can add clip art to a slide that has a clip art placeholder or a Content placeholder on it.

◆ Open the City Music Store presentation file, and display the Student Instruments slide.

Basic steps

1 Double-click on the **clip art** placeholder

Or

2 Click on the **Insert clip art** icon within the **Content** placeholder graphic

3 At the **Select Picture** dialog box, enter a keyword to indicate what you are looking for and click [Go]

4 Scroll through the clip art until you find one you want to use

5 Select it and click [OK]

The clip art will appear on your slide. It will be selected, and the Picture toolbar will be displayed

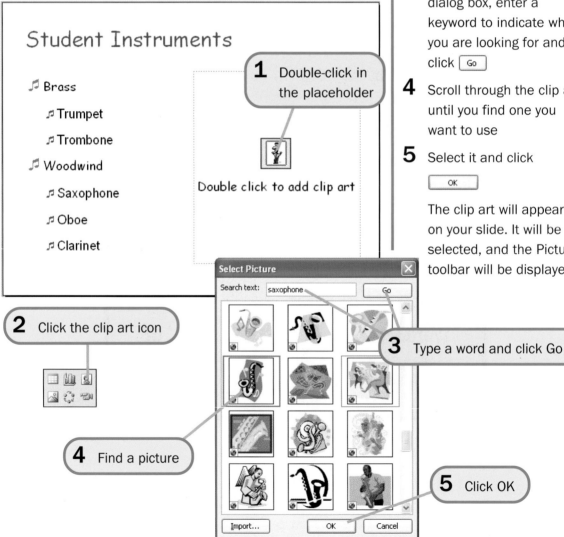

Formatting clip art

1 Select the object – click on it – then drag it into its new position

■ **To resize clip art**

2 Select the object, then drag one of the 'handles' – the circles in each corner and on each edge

■ **To specify an exact size**

3 Select the object and click **Format Picture** on the **Picture** toolbar

4 Display the **Size** tab

5 Set the **Height** and **Width** as required

6 Set the **Scaling** options (see below)

7 Click [OK]

■ Insert suitable clip art on slide 3 in the City Music Store file. Move and resize it as you wish.

You can move or resize the clip art to get the effect you want on your slide.

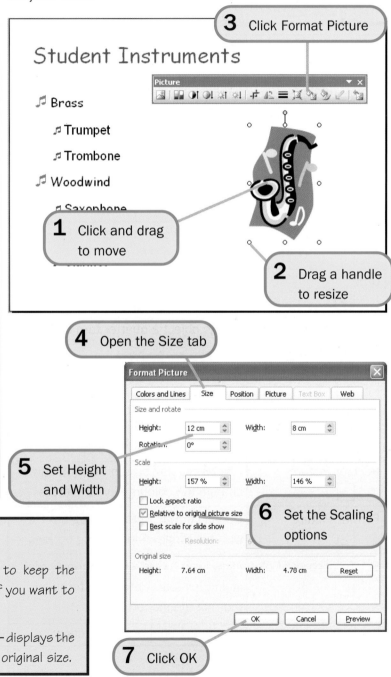

Scaling options

Lock aspect ratio – turn on to keep the picture in proportion. Turn off if you want to be able to distort the object.

Relative to original picture size – displays the current scaling, relative to the original size.

Picture toolbar

Insert Picture	Opens Insert Picture dialog box so you can insert a picture from a file
Image Control	Options are Automatic, Greyscale, Black & White and Washout.
More Contrast	Increase the contrast between the colours and shades
Less Contrast	Decrease the contrast between the colours and shades
More Brightness	Increase the brightness of the picture
Less Brightness	Decrease the brightness of the picture
Crop	Click, then position over handle on corner or edge of picture, and drag
Rotate left 90°	Rotate object a quarter turn to the left
Line Style	Select a line style to give the object a border
Compress Pictures	Reduces size of pictures so the file takes up less space on disk
Recolor Picture	Displays dialog box so that you can change the colours in your picture
Format Picture	Opens Format Picture dialog box with full range of formatting options
Set Transparent Color	Allows you to set a transparent area in your picture – available for most (but not all) file formats
Reset Picture	Resets the picture to its original state

Take note

If the Picture toolbar does not appear when you select a clip art object, open the View menu, choose Toolbars then click Picture.

Tip

You can also insert images from files, e.g. a .bmp or .jpg file. Choose Picture from the Insert menu and then select From File. At the Insert Picture dialog box, browse to locate the file, select it and click Insert.

Selecting objects

The various tools on the Drawing toolbar can be used to customize and add interest to your slides. The **Select objects** tool ⬜ is used to select objects. Once selected, they can be moved, resized, formatted or deleted. The tool is always active unless you pick another tool from the Drawing toolbar.

■ **To select a text object**

Click on any text within the area. Note the handles that appear at the corners and on the edges of the selected object.

■ **To select other objects**

Click anywhere inside the object placeholder

■ **To deselect an object**

Click anywhere outside the selected object.

■ **To move**

Click on the border of a text object, or anywhere within other types and drag into position.

■ **To resize**

Drag one of the handles (note the double-headed pointer) until the object is the required size.

■ **To delete a text object**

Select it, click the border once, and press [**Delete**].

■ **To delete other objects**

Select, and press [**Delete**].

◆ The Drawing toolbar is normally displayed along the bottom of the PowerPoint window. If it is not displayed, open the View menu, choose Toolbars, then Drawing.

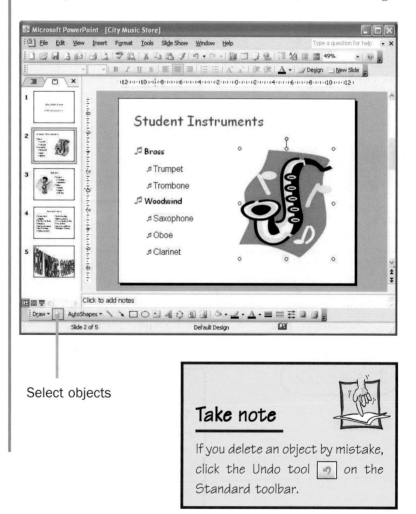

Select objects

Take note

If you delete an object by mistake, click the Undo tool ↺ on the Standard toolbar.

Drawing tools

The line, arrow, rectangle and oval tools all work in a similar way. You can customize the shapes in many ways – add a shadow or 3-D effect, change the line colour and thickness, or change fill colours and patterns.

◆ Add a blank slide to the end of your City Music Store presentation and experiment with the drawing tools.

- **Line-based tools**

1 Select a tool – line, arrow, rectangle or oval

2 Click to set the start

3 Drag to draw the shape

Hold **[Shift]** as you drag to get a straight line (Line tool), square (Rectangle tool) or circle (Oval tool)

- **To format the object**

4 Select the object

5 Use the formatting tools on the drawing toolbar to set its colours, style or to add a shadow or 3-D effect

6 De-select the object

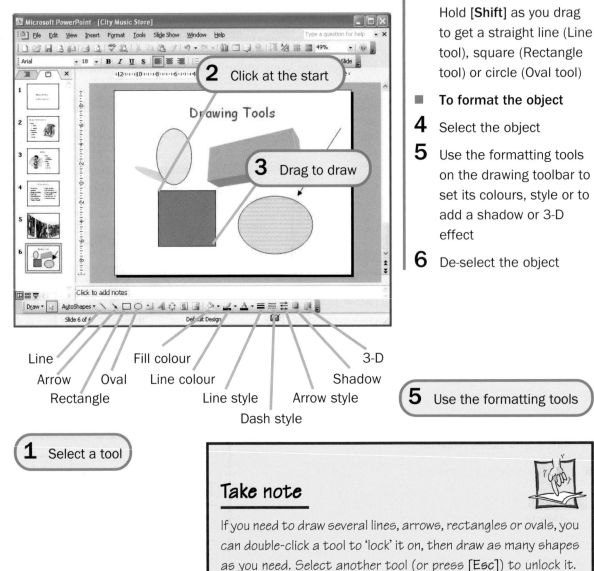

2 Click at the start

3 Drag to draw

Line
Arrow   Oval   Line colour
Rectangle   Fill colour
Line style   Arrow style   Shadow   3-D
Dash style

5 Use the formatting tools

1 Select a tool

Take note

If you need to draw several lines, arrows, rectangles or ovals, you can double-click a tool to 'lock' it on, then draw as many shapes as you need. Select another tool (or press **[Esc]**) to unlock it.

Basic steps

1 Click the **AutoShapes** tool to list the categories

2 Select a category

3 Choose a shape

4 Click and drag to draw the object on the slide

5 Drag the yellow adjust handle to alter the shape

■ **Freeform**

6 Click and drag (note the pencil shaped pointer) to draw lines freehand

Or, to get a straight line

7 Click where you want the line to start, then click again where it will end

■ **Curve**

8 Click a path that you want the curve to follow

9 Double-click or press [**Esc**] when done to switch the tool off

You may find the shape you need under AutoShapes. If you want stars, triangles, arrows, etc. on your slide you'll find lots to choose from. AutoShapes can be drawn and formatted in the same way as the basic drawing shapes.

◆ The Freeform and Curve AutoShapes in the Line category don't quite follow the basic 'click and drag' principle adopted by the other drawing tools.

Experiment with the various options.

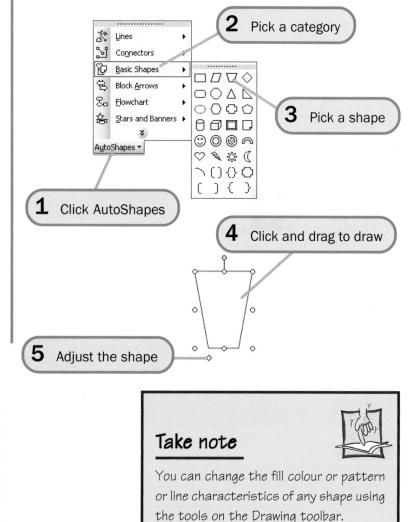

2 Pick a category

3 Pick a shape

1 Click AutoShapes

4 Click and drag to draw

5 Adjust the shape

Tip

To select a drawing object, click anywhere within it.

Take note

You can change the fill colour or pattern or line characteristics of any shape using the tools on the Drawing toolbar.

More AutoShapes

Additional shapes can also be found in the More AutoShapes category, or online.

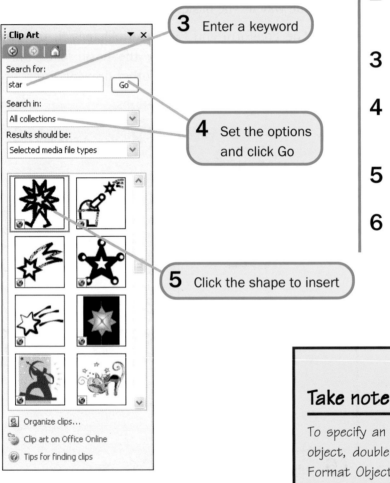

3 Enter a keyword

4 Set the options and click Go

5 Click the shape to insert

1 Select **More AutoShapes** from the **AutoShapes** list

2 Connect to the Internet when prompted (if necesary)

3 Enter a keyword in the clip art task pane

4 Select the search collections and results options and click Go

5 Click on the shape that you want to insert

6 Move and/or resize the shape as required

Take note

To specify an exact size for a drawing object, double-click on it to open the Format Object dialog box, and set the sizes on the Size tab.

Basic Steps

1 Select the object

2 Choose **Rotate or Flip** from the **Draw** menu

3 Select an option from the submenu – the **Rotate** options turn the object 90° right or left, the **Flip** options turn it 180°

4 With the **Free Rotate** tool, drag a rotate handle to turn the shape the way you want

Rotate or Flip

Once an object has been drawn, you can flip it over horizontally or vertically, or rotate it right or left to get the effect you want.

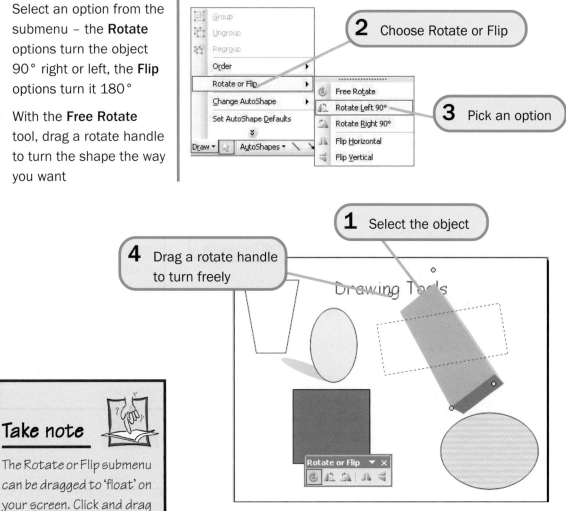

2 Choose Rotate or Flip

3 Pick an option

1 Select the object

4 Drag a rotate handle to turn freely

Take note

The Rotate or Flip submenu can be dragged to 'float' on your screen. Click and drag its title bar. Any submenu with a title bar can become a floating menu.

Changing the order

When you draw objects onto your slides, they lie in layers relative to the order in which they are drawn. The first object is on the bottom layer, the next one on a layer above the first one and so on.

Using this layering principle, you can create complex drawings by overlapping objects one on top of another.

If you need to rearrange the layering of your objects, you can do so using the Bring Forward and Send Backward commands.

Basic steps

1 Select the object you wish to Bring Forward or Send Backward

2 Open the **Draw** menu

3 Select **Order**

4 Choose the order option required

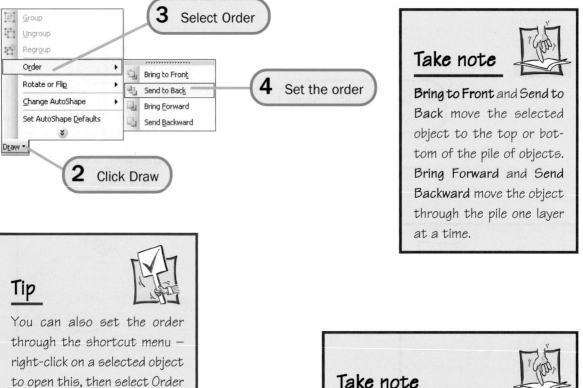

3 Select Order

2 Click Draw

4 Set the order

Group
Ungroup
Regroup
Order
Rotate or Flip
Change AutoShape
Set AutoShape Defaults
Draw

Bring to Front
Send to Back
Bring Forward
Send Backward

Take note

Bring to Front and **Send to Back** move the selected object to the top or bottom of the pile of objects. **Bring Forward** and **Send Backward** move the object through the pile one layer at a time.

Tip

You can also set the order through the shortcut menu – right-click on a selected object to open this, then select Order and specify the option required.

Take note

To align objects on a slide, e.g. by their top, bottom or middle, use the **Align** or **Distribute** options in the Draw menu.

66

Group and Ungroup

Basic steps

1 Select the objects to group – click on the first then hold **[Shift]** down and click on the others

2 Open the **Draw** menu

3 Select **Group**

■ **To edit a grouped object**

4 Select the group

5 Use **Draw > Ungroup** to split it into its objects, which can then be edited

If you have drawn several objects to generate an image, you can group the objects together into one to make it easier to move, copy or resize the whole image.

Take note

To add text to a drawing object, right-click on it, select **Add Text** from the context menu, then type your text inside the object.

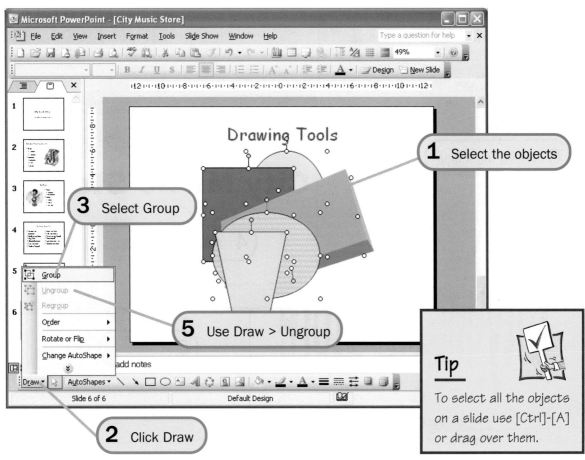

1 Select the objects

3 Select Group

5 Use Draw > Ungroup

2 Click Draw

Tip

To select all the objects on a slide use [Ctrl]-[A] or drag over them.

WordArt

You can use WordArt to create special text effects on your slides. It allows you to produce stunning title sides and real eye-catchers wherever they are needed.

◆ Add a blank slide to the end of the City Music Store file.

Basic steps

1 Click the **Insert WordArt** tool 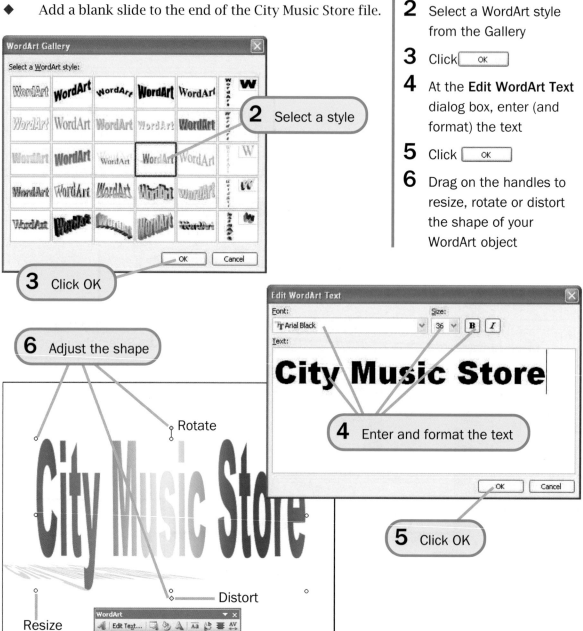 on the Drawing toolbar

2 Select a WordArt style from the Gallery

3 Click OK

4 At the **Edit WordArt Text** dialog box, enter (and format) the text

5 Click OK

6 Drag on the handles to resize, rotate or distort the shape of your WordArt object

WordArt Gallery

Select a WordArt style:

2 Select a style

3 Click OK

6 Adjust the shape

Rotate

Edit WordArt Text

Font: Arial Black   Size: 36 **B** *I*

Text:

City Music Store

4 Enter and format the text

5 Click OK

Distort

Resize

WordArt ▾ × | Edit Text...

68

WordArt toolbar

Insert WordArt	Inserts a WordArt object
Edit Text	Opens the dialog box so you can edit and/or format the text
Gallery	Displays the WordArt gallery so you can choose a different style
Format WordArt	Opens Format WordArt dialog box that contains full range of formatting options
Shape	Displays alternative WordArt shapes available
Same letter heights	Toggles the same height option of upper and lower case letters
Vertical Text	Rotates the text vertically
Alignment	Displays list of alignment and justification options
Character spacing	Displays list of character spacing options

Alignment options: Left Align, Center, Right Align, Word Justify, Letter Justify, Stretch Justify

Character spacing options: Very Tight, Tight, Normal, Loose, Very Loose, Custom: 100 %, Kern Character Pairs

Exercises

A: City Music Store

1 Open the City Music Store file.

2 On slide 2, flip the image horizontally.

3 On the title slide, create the following object:

Add a 6 cm by 6 cm square to the top right of the slide. Set its fill colour to red and its line style to 4½.

Add a triangle (AutoShapes, Basic Shapes). Place it on top of the square, and resize it to the same width and height. Set its the fill colour to dark blue.

Add a star (AutoShapes, Stars and Banners). Position it on top of the other objects, and resize it to the same width and height. Set its fill colour to yellow.

Group the objects, and resize the group to 4 cm by 4 cm.

4 Flip the object vertically.

5 Align the object to the top right of the slide.

6 Ungroup the object on the Title slide and recolour the individual objects as you wish. Regroup the object.

The City Music Store file should look similar to this

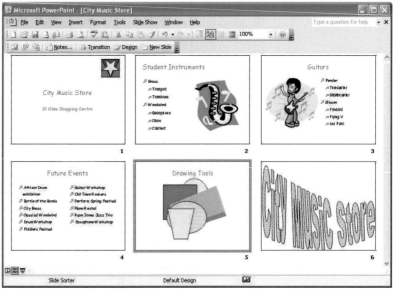

70

7 Save and close your file.

B: Westside Sports

1 Open the Westside Sports presentation file.

2 Add a suitable piece of clip art to slide 2, resize it to 12 cm high and 9 cm wide, and reposition it if necessary.

3 Add a new, blank slide to the end of the presentation

4 Using WordArt, add an object that says 'Westside Sports'. Set the text size to 72, with upper and lower case letters the same height. Reposition it in the middle of the slide.

5 Using the drawing tools, create a logo in the upper right corner similar to the illustration here, on this slide only.

6 Group the objects, then resize it to 5 cm high and 6 wide.

7 Use the align options to position the logo on the slide.

8 Save and close your file.

The Westside Sports file should look similar to this

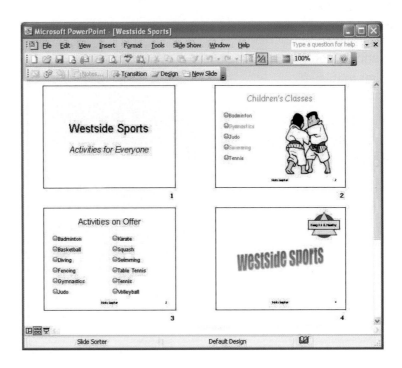

C: Creatures of the Deep

1 Open the Creatures of the Deep presentation file.

2 Add a suitable piece of clip art to slide 2.

3 Resize the clip art object to 9 cm high and 12 cm wide. and reposition it if necessary.

4 Add a new blank slide to the end of the file.

5 Add a WordArt object, with the text 'Creatures of the Deep', setting the size to 66.

6 Reposition the object if necessary.

7 Use the drawing tools to create a logo on the bottom right of this slide. Use at least two different drawing objects and add some text.

8 Save and close your file.

The Creatures of the Deep file should now look similar to this:

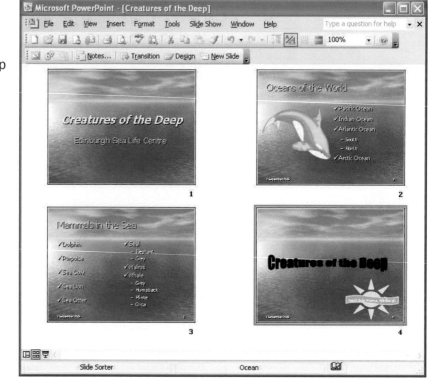

5 Tables and charts

Tables

If you are accustomed to creating tables using Word, you'll find it very easy to create tables on your slides.

There are several ways to do it. We will consider:

◆ Using a slide with a Table placeholder set up

◆ Using a slide with a Contents placeholder

◆ Drawing a table onto a slide

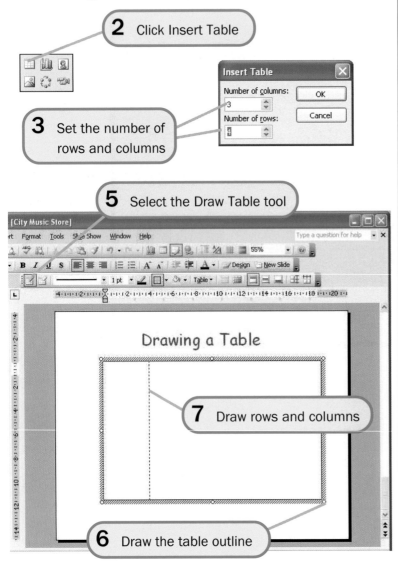

2 Click Insert Table

3 Set the number of rows and columns

5 Select the Draw Table tool

Drawing a Table

7 Draw rows and columns

6 Draw the table outline

■ **To use a placeholder**

1 Double-click the **Table** placeholder

Or

2 Click the **Insert Table** tool in a **Contents** placeholder

3 Specify the number of rows and columns and click [OK]

■ **To draw a table**

4 Click the **Tables and Borders** tool on the Standard toolbar to display the Tables and Borders toolbar

5 The **Draw Table** tool should be selected (if not, click on it now).

6 Click and drag to draw a rectangle the size you want your table to be

7 Draw rows and columns where you want them

8 Switch the **Draw Table** tool off – click or press [**Esc**]

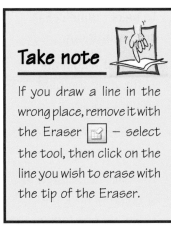

The Tables and Borders toolbar

Draw table	Select this tool, then drag on your slide to create your table
Eraser	Click on a line or border to erase it
Border style	Apply the current style or click the arrow to display the styles options
Border width	Apply the current width or click the arrow to display the width options
Border color	Apply the current colour or click the arrow to displays the colour options
Borders	Switch borders on and off. Click the drop-down arrow to display options
Fill color	Adds the current background colour to the selected cells. Click the drop-down arrow to display options
Table options	Click the down arrow to display options for inserting/deleting rows/columns, etc.
Merge cells	Select the cells to be merged, then click the Merge Cells tool
Split cell	Splits the selected cell
Vertical alignment	Select the cell(s), then click an option – top, centre or bottom of cell
Distribute rows evenly	Adjusts row heights of selected rows so that they are equal
Distribute columns evenly	Adjusts column widths of selected columns so that they are equal

Working in a table

Moving around

- Press **[Tab]** to move to the next cell
- Press **[Shift]-[Tab]** to go to the previous cell

Or

- Use the arrow keys to move up, down, right and left

Or

- Click in the cell you wish to work on.

Click outside your table when you've finished working on it (the Tables and Borders toolbar will disappear).

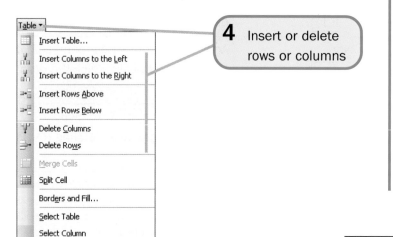

4 Insert or delete rows or columns

1 To select table cells, drag over them

2 To adjust a column width, drag the right column border

3 To adjust a row height, drag the lower border

4 To insert or delete a row or column, click the **Table** options tool on the **Table and Borders** toolbar and select the option required (you will need to adjust the column width/row height to get a good fit)

5 To resize rows and/or columns so that they are the same height/width, select them, and then use **Distribute Rows Evenly** ⊞ or **Distribute Columns Evenly** ⊞

Tip

Use the Formatting and Table and Borders toolbars to format your data. Experiment with the options.

Basic steps

- **Using a Chart placeholder**

1 Double-click the placeholder

- **Using a Content placeholder**

2 Click the **Insert Chart** tool in the **Content** placeholder

If you have figures to present, and you feel that they will be displayed more effectively using a chart rather than a table, you will find that the charting feature in PowerPoint is very comprehensive.

There are several ways to create a chart on a slide. We will consider:

◆   Using a slide with a Chart placeholder

Or

◆   Using a slide with a Content placeholder.

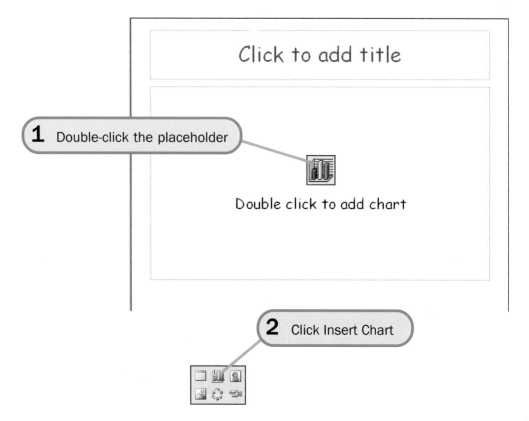

Click to add title

1 Double-click the placeholder

Double click to add chart

2 Click Insert Chart

Chart window

When the chart window is displayed, there will be a default chart within it.

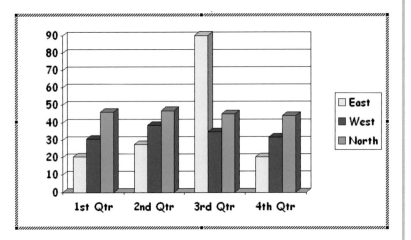

There is also a small Datasheet window (which can be moved or resized as necessary), where you can key in the data that you want to chart.

		A	B	C	D	E
		1st Qtr	2nd Qtr	3rd Qtr	4th Qtr	
1	East	20.4	27.4	90	20.4	
2	West	30.6	38.6	34.6	31.6	
3	North	45.9	46.9	45	43.9	

City Music Store - Datasheet

The Standard and Formatting toolbars are modified to contain some tools that are used when working with charts, and you will notice a Chart menu appear on the Menu bar. The options available in the other menus also change to present options suitable for working on charts.

◆   Explore the menus to see how they have changed.

Basic steps

1 Select the cell into which you wish to enter your own data

2 Key in the data

3 Move to the next cell you want to work on – use any of the methods suggested

■ **To delete unwanted cells**

4 Right-click on the column letter or row number of the one you wish to delete and select the **Delete** option in the shortcut menu

To display your own data, simply replace the sample data in the Datasheet window with the data you want to chart.

If you do not need to replace all the sample data, you can delete the columns or rows that are not required.

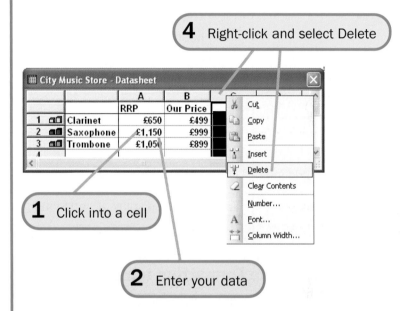

4 Right-click and select Delete

1 Click into a cell

2 Enter your data

City Music Store - Datasheet

		A	B
		RRP	Our Price
1	Clarinet	£650	£499
2	Saxophone	£1,150	£999
3	Trombone	£1,050	£899

Shortcut menu: Cut, Copy, Paste, Insert, Delete, Clear Contents, Number..., Font..., Column Width...

Moving around your datasheet

There are a number of ways to move from cell to cell within the Datasheet. You can use the:

Arrow keys one cell in direction of arrow

[Tab] forward to the next cell

[Shift]-[Tab] back to the previous cell

[Enter] down to the next cell in a column

Or

Point to the cell and click.

The cell you are in (your current cell) has a dark border.

Take note

Don't enter too much data – the chart will be seen on a slide or over-head. If it's too detailed your audience may not fully appreciate it.

Chart tools on the Standard toolbar

Chart object	Value Axis	Selects individual objects within your chart
Format object		Opens a Format dialog box so that you can format the selected object
View datasheet		Toggles the display of the datasheet
By row		The row headings appear in the legend – a graphic in the row heading of your datasheet indicates the selected option
By column		The column labels are in the legend – a graphic in the column heading of your datasheet indicates the selected option
Data table		Toggles the display of the data table
Chart type		Displays list of alternative chart types to choose from
Category axis gridlines		Toggles display of vertical gridlines
Value axis gridlines		Toggles display of horizontal gridlines
Legend		Toggles display of legend

Chart tools on the Formatting toolbar

Currency style		Displays the selected data on the datasheet with a £ symbol and 2 decimal places, e.g. £1,565.75
Percent style		Displays the selected data on the datasheet as a percentage, e.g. 150%
Comma style		Displays the selected data on the datasheet with commas as the thousand and million dividers and 2 decimal places, e.g. 1,565.75
Increase decimal		Increases the number of decimal places in the selected cells
Decrease decimal		Decreases the number of decimal places in the selected cells
Angle clockwise		Formats selected text on chart e.g. Category axis or chart title
Angle counter-clockwise		Formats selected text on chart e.g. Category axis or chart title

Basic steps

- **To select from standard chart types**

1 Click the drop-down arrow to display the chart types available

2 Choose one

- **To select from full range**

3 Open the **Chart** menu and choose **Chart Type...**

4 Select the **Standard Types** tab

5 Explore the options available – select a **type** then a **sub-type**

6 Hold down the **Press and Hold to View Sample** button to display a preview of your chart

7 Click OK

The standard chart type is the Column Chart. You can choose from a wide range of chart types, but the ones that are probably best suited to the data that you are likely to be charting at this stage are the Bar, Column or Line chart types.

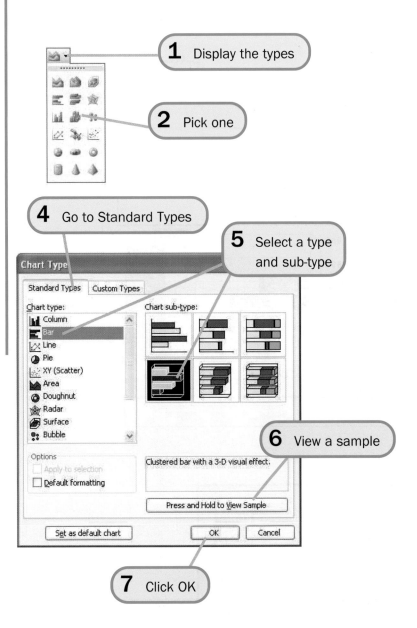

1 Display the types

2 Pick one

4 Go to Standard Types

5 Select a type and sub-type

6 View a sample

7 Click OK

Hiding rows and columns

You may have entered data into your datasheet, and then decide that you don't wish to display the data on the chart. If you don't want to delete the data, you can hide it. You can then unhide it when you wish to display it, rather than have to type it in again.

1 Display the datasheet if necessary

2 Double-click on the heading – the letter at the top – of the column you wish to hide

Or

Double-click the row number to the left of the row you wish to hide – the data is dimmed and will not appear on the chart.

3 To reveal the data again double-click on the column heading or row number.

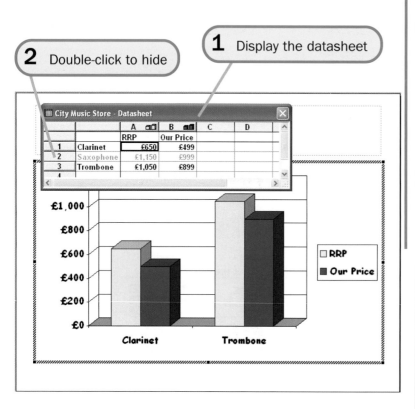

2 Double-click to hide

1 Display the datasheet

Take note

Click outside the chart placeholder when you have completed your chart.

Take note

To edit a chart, double-click on it to display the toolbars, chart menu and datasheet again.

Chart objects

Basic steps

■ To format an object

1 Select it – click on it on the chart

Or

2 Select it from the **Chart Object** list `Value Axis  ▼`

3 Click the **Format Object** tool 📄 on the Standard toolbar

Or

4 Double-click on the object that you wish to format – the **Format** dialog box for that object will be displayed

5 Set your options and click `OK`

Each part of your chart is an object in its own right. The chart objects are:

Category axis	Chart area	Corners
Floor	Legend	Plot area
Value axis	Value axis	Major grid lines
Wall	Series	

Use the Chart Objects tool to help you learn what each object is called. Select an object from the drop-down list, and have a look at your chart to see what has been selected – take a tour of the objects!

You can format each object on your chart in a variety of ways. The formatting options vary from object to object.

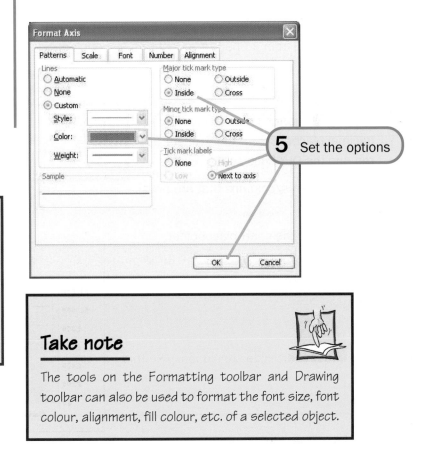

Tip

Explore the dialog box and experiment with the formatting options that are available.

Take note

The tools on the Formatting toolbar and Drawing toolbar can also be used to format the font size, font colour, alignment, fill colour, etc. of a selected object.

Exercises

A: City Music Store

1 Open the City Music Store file.

2 Add a new slide at the end of the file with either a Table or a Contents placeholder and create a table that has three columns and four rows.

3 Add the slide title 'Discounted Prices'.

4 Complete the table showing the recommended retail prices (RRP) and City Music Store (Our) prices.

5 Centre the column headings and right-align the figures.

6 Save your file.

7 Add another new slide at the end of the file and insert a chart starting from a Chart or a Contents placeholder.

8 Add the slide title 'Price Comparison' and enter the data as shown.

9 Format the figures to currency, with no decimal places. Colour the RRP series red and the Our Price series yellow

10 Delete the rows/columns that are not required.

11 Click outside the chart placeholder.

12 Save and close your file.

Discounted Prices

	RRP	Our Price
Clarinet	£650	£499
Saxophone	£1150	£999
Trombone	£1050	£899

City Music Store - Datasheet

		A ⊞ RRP	B ⊞ Our Price	C	D
1	Clarinet	£650	£499		
2	Saxophone	£1,150	£999		
3	Trombone	£1,050	£899		
4					

Your chart slide should look like this

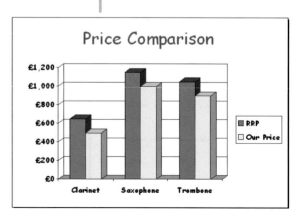

B: Westside Sports

1 Open the Westside Sports file.

2 Add a new slide 3, with a Table or Contents placeholder and create a table, four columns by four rows

3 Enter 'Class Times' as the slide title, and the class time data as shown.

4 Adjust the column widths if necessary.

5 Centre the column headings and the sports horizontally in each cell and centre the data in all cells vertically

6 Save your file.

7 Add a new slide 4 with either a Chart or a Contents placeholder and create a chart.

8 Enter 'Class Numbers' as the slide title

9 Enter the number of children taking each sport into the chart datasheet

10 Display the data By Column.

11 The Chart Type should be a 2-D column chart.

12 Move the Legend to the top of the chart.

13 Display the Data Table.

14 Save and close your file.

Your chart slide should look like this

Class Times

	4-5 pm	5-6 pm	6-7 pm
Monday	Gymnastics	Swimming	Judo
Wednesday	Swimming	Tennis	Gymnastics
Friday	Badminton	Judo	Badminton

Moira Stephen — 3

Westside Sports - Datasheet

		A	B	C	D
		2005	2006		
1	Badminton	40	54		
2	Gymnastics	52	64		
3	Judo	30	45		
4	Swimming	60	75		
5					

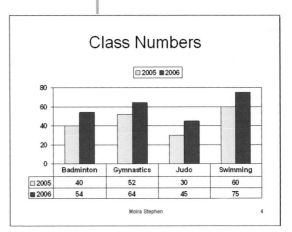

Class Numbers

☐ 2005 ■ 2006

	Badminton	Gymnastics	Judo	Swimming
☐ 2005	40	52	30	60
■ 2006	54	64	45	75

Moira Stephen — 4

C: Creatures of the Deep

1 Open the Creatures of the Deep file.

2 Add a new slide 4, with a Table or Contents placeholder and create a table, two columns by six rows. Enter the latest sightings data.

3 Enter 'Latest sightings' in the title area.

4 Adjust the column widths if necessary.

5 Save your file.

6 Add a new slide at the end of the presentation with a Chart or Contents placeholder and create a chart.

7 Add 'Number of Visitors' in the slide title area.

8 Create a graph to display the number of visitor data.

9 Delete any sample rows/columns not required.

10 Set the chart type to a line graph, and move the Legend to the bottom of the chart.

11 Change the colour and weight of the lines.

12 Save your file.

Your chart slide should look like this

Latest sightings

10th August	12 Harbour Porpoises
22nd July	5 Killer Whales
3rd July	Basking Shark
1st July	3 Killer Whales
29th June	2 White Sided Dolphins
27th June	Minke Whales

Creatures of the Deep - Datasheet

		A	B	C
		2005	2006	
1	Adult	450	580	
2	Child	980	1200	
3	Concession	750	900	

Number of Visitors

6 Organization Charts

Creating a chart

Organization charts give you another opportunity to make your point using a diagram rather than words. They are designed to show staff structures, but can be used for other types of hierarchies. There are several ways to create an organization chart. We will consider:

◆ Using a slide with an Organization Chart placeholder

◆ Using a slide with a Contents placeholder

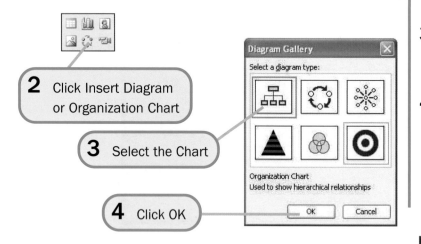

2 Click Insert Diagram or Organization Chart

3 Select the Chart

4 Click OK

Diagram Gallery

Select a diagram type:

Organization Chart
Used to show hierarchical relationships

OK   Cancel

1 Double-click in an **Organization Chart** placeholder

Or

2 Click the **Insert Diagram or Organization Chart** tool in a **Contents** placeholder

3 Select **Organization Chart** from the **Diagram Gallery** dialog box

4 Click [OK] – an organization chart object will be displayed. You will see a set of shapes and the Organization Chart toolbar.

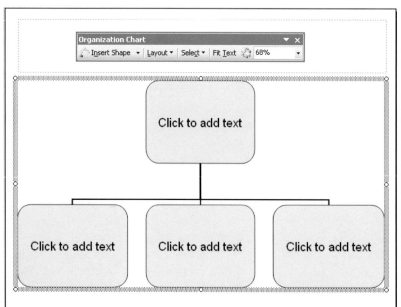

Organization Chart

Insert Shape ▾ | Layout ▾ | Select ▾ | Fit Text | 68% ▾

Click to add text

Click to add text   Click to add text   Click to add text

Tip

Work out the structure you wish to display before you start. A few minutes spent sketching it out on paper could save you time redrawing and correcting it on-screen.

Don't try to display too large a structure – the finished slide should be clear and easily understood.

Adding and editing text

Basic steps

- **To add text**

1 Click in the shape and key in your data – press **[Enter]** to create a new row if you have more than one line of data for the shape

2 Click on the next shape or outside the shape, when you are finished

- **To edit text**

3 Click within the shape

4 Move the insertion point if necessary then insert (just type) or delete text as required

---

Adding and editing text to the shapes in an organization chart couldn't be easier – just follow the instructions on the screen!

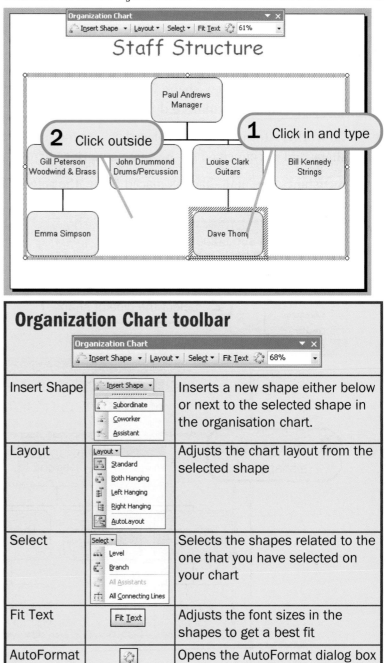

Organization Chart toolbar

Insert Shape	Insert Shape ▾ / Subordinate / Coworker / Assistant	Inserts a new shape either below or next to the selected shape in the organisation chart.
Layout	Layout ▾ / Standard / Both Hanging / Left Hanging / Right Hanging / AutoLayout	Adjusts the chart layout from the selected shape
Select	Select ▾ / Level / Branch / All Assistants / All Connecting Lines	Selects the shapes related to the one that you have selected on your chart
Fit Text	Fit Text	Adjusts the font sizes in the shapes to get a best fit
AutoFormat		Opens the AutoFormat dialog box

89

Adjusting the structure

You can adjust the structure of your chart by adding, deleting or moving shapes. Additional shapes must be related to an existing shape.

There are three types of relationship to choose from – subordinate, co-worker and assistant.

◆ **Subordinate** – the new shape will be placed below the selected shape and connected to it

◆ **Co-worker** – the new shape is placed next to the selected shape and is connected to the same superior shape

◆ **Assistant** – the new shape is placed below the selected shape with an elbow connector.

■ **To add a shape**

1 Click the shape that you wish to relate a new shape to

2 Click **Insert Shape** to insert a **Subordinate** box

Or

3 Click the down arrow to the right of the **Insert Shape** tool on the Organization Chart toolbar and select the type of shape

■ **To delete a shape**

4 Click on the edge of the shape to select it

5 Press [**Delete**]

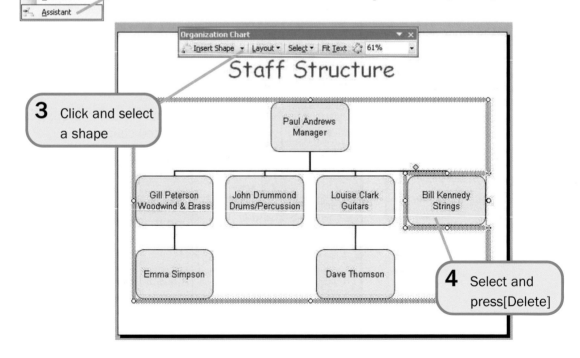

1 Click to add a subordinate

2 Select the type of shape

3 Click and select a shape

4 Select and press[Delete]

Staff Structure

Paul Andrews Manager

Gill Peterson Woodwind & Brass

John Drummond Drums/Percussion

Louise Clark Guitars

Bill Kennedy Strings

Emma Simpson

Dave Thomson

Formatting

There are a number of formatting options to choose from when working on your chart. You can change the layout, or format the shapes manually, using the tools on the Formatting and Drawing toolbars, or select an AutoFormat.

- **To adjust the layout**

1 Select a superior shape – one with subordinates

2 Click the **Layout** button on the Organization Chart toolbar

3 Select a layout option

- **To format a box or a line**

4 Select the object then use the formatting tools on the **Drawing** toolbar, e.g. Line Style, Line Color, Fill, Shadow, etc.

- **To format text**

5 Select the text then use the tools on the **Formatting** toolbar, e.g. Font size, Color, Bold, etc.

- **To use AutoFormat**

6 Click the **AutoFormat** tool on the Organization Chart toolbar

7 Select an AutoFormat

8 Click [OK]

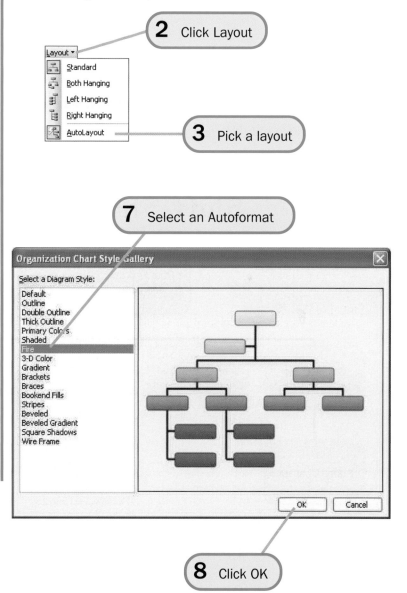

91

Exercises

A: City Music Store

1 Open the City Music Store presentation.

2 Add a new slide after slide 3 with either an Organization Chart or Contents placeholder.

3 Enter 'Staff Structure' as the slide title.

4 Create the following organisation chart.

5 Format your chart using one of the AutoFormat options.

6 Save and close your file.

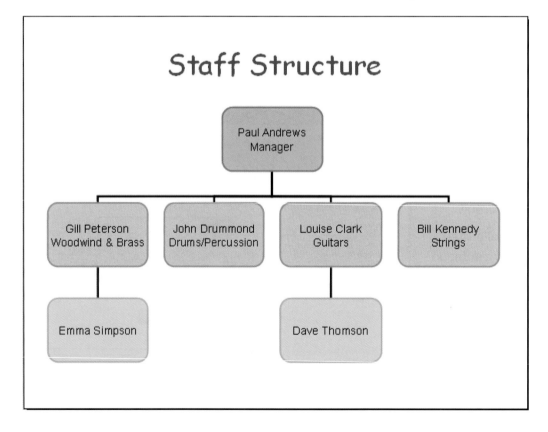

B: Westside Sports

1 Open the Westside Sports presentation.

2 Add a new slide at the end of the file.

3 Give the slide the title 'Coaching Staff'.

4 Enter the following data into your organisation chart.

5 Format the chart using one of the AutoFormat options.

6 Make all the staff names bold.

7 Save and close your file.

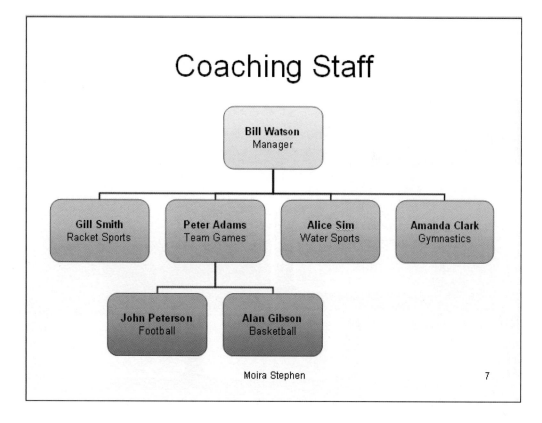

C: Creatures of the Deep

1 Open the Creatures of the Deep presentation.

2 Add a new slide after slide 1.

3 Give the slide the title 'Administrative Staff'.

4 Enter the following data into your organisation chart.

5 Format the line style of the shapes to 6 pt.

6 Change the colour and weight of the lines joining the shapes.

7 Save and close your file.

7 Slide show preparation

Notes

If you are delivering a presentation, you will most likely use notes for some (or all) of your slides to help you remember all the things that you want to say when the slide is displayed. The Notes feature allows you to type and edit the notes that accompany each slide, and you can print them out so that you can refer to them during your presentation as required.

You can add notes to your slides in Normal or in Slide Sorter view.

■ **In Normal view**

1 Display the slide you wish to make notes for

2 Click in the Notes pane

3 Enter and edit your notes as required

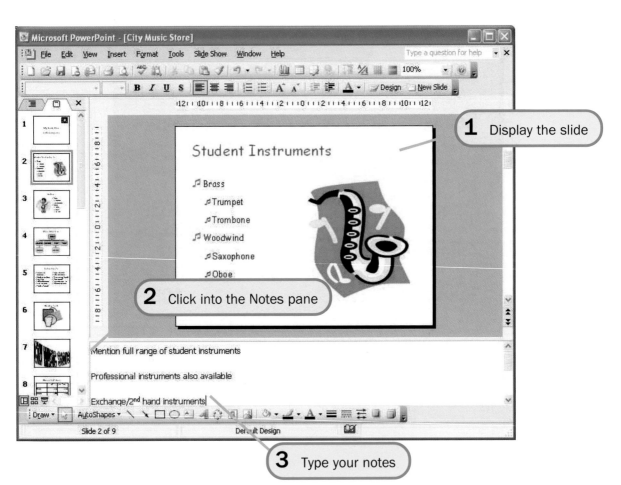

Basic steps

■ **In Slide Sorter view**

1 Select the slide you wish to make notes for

2 Click the [Notes...] tool on the Slide Sorter toolbar

3 Enter and edit your notes in the **Speaker Notes** window

4 Click [Close]

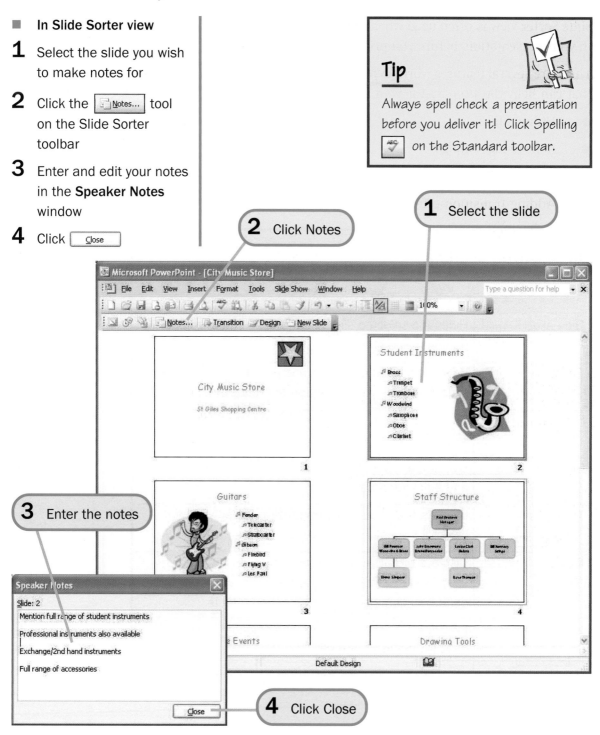

2 Click Notes

1 Select the slide

3 Enter the notes

4 Click Close

Slide Sorter view

Slide Sorter view is often used when putting the final touches to your presentation, before you print or deliver it on screen.

There are several features worth exploring in Slide Sorter view that can help you prepare for your slide show, including:

◆   Hiding slides

◆   Rehearsing timings

◆   Creating a summary slide

◆   Adding transition effects.

Take note

The features discussed in this chapter can also be found in the Slide Show menu.

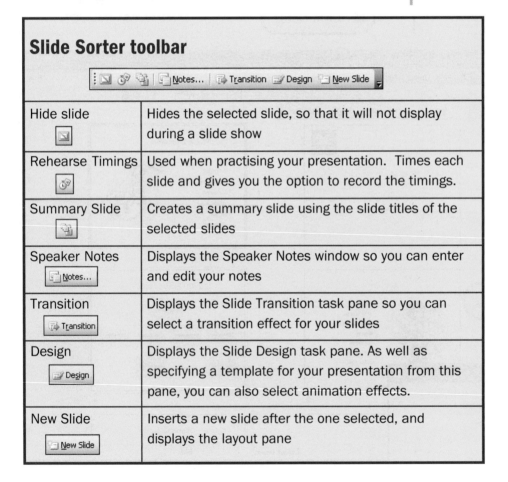

Slide Sorter toolbar

Hide slide	Hides the selected slide, so that it will not display during a slide show
Rehearse Timings	Used when practising your presentation. Times each slide and gives you the option to record the timings.
Summary Slide	Creates a summary slide using the slide titles of the selected slides
Speaker Notes	Displays the Speaker Notes window so you can enter and edit your notes
Transition	Displays the Slide Transition task pane so you can select a transition effect for your slides
Design	Displays the Slide Design task pane. As well as specifying a template for your presentation from this pane, you can also select animation effects.
New Slide	Inserts a new slide after the one selected, and displays the layout pane

Hide Slide

Basic steps

- **To hide a slide**
1 Select the slide
2 Click ⬚ the **Hide Slide** tool – the slide number is crossed out

- **To remove hidden status**
3 Select the slide
4 Click the **Hide Slide** tool

This option can prove useful if you're not sure whether or not you will really need a particular slide for your presentation. You can include the slide in your presentation (in case it's needed), but hide it. The hidden slide will be bypassed during your slide show, unless you decide you need to use it after all.

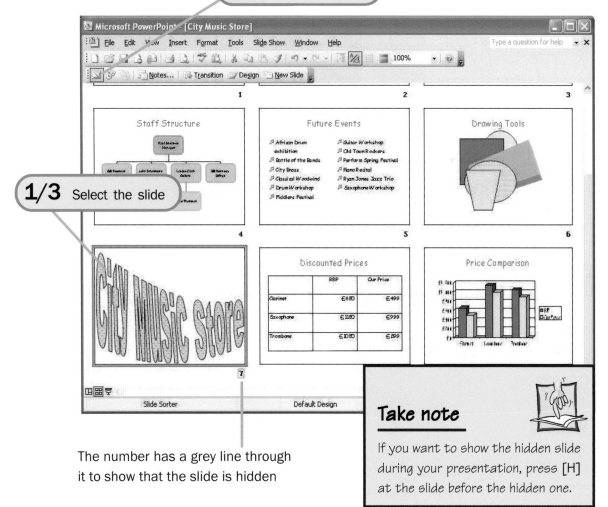

2/4 Click Hide Slide

1/3 Select the slide

The number has a grey line through it to show that the slide is hidden

Take note

If you want to show the hidden slide during your presentation, press [H] at the slide before the hidden one.

Rehearse Timings

It is a very good idea to practise your presentation before you end up in front of your audience. As well as practising what you intend to say (probably with the aid of notes you have made using the Speaker's Notes feature), you can rehearse the timings for each slide.

1 Select the slide you want to start your presentation from (usually the first)

2 Click the **Rehearse Timings** tool ⟨🔄⟩ to do your practice run

3 Go over what you intend to say while the slide is displayed

4 Click the left mouse button to move to the next slide when ready

5 Repeat steps 3 and 4 until you reach the end of your presentation

Rehearsal toolbar

Rehearsal ▼ ×	
⇨ ‖ 0:00:25 ↺ 0:04:19	
Next ⇨	Moves onto next slide in presentation
Pause ‖	Pauses the slide show. Click the tool again to restart it from same point.
Slide Time 0:00:25	Displays the time spent on the current slide
Repeat ↺	Restarts the timing for the current slide
Total presentation time 0:04:19	Displays the total time taken on the presentation

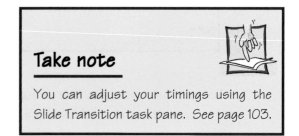

Take note

You can adjust your timings using the Slide Transition task pane. See page 103.

Displaying timings

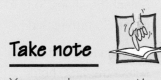
A dialog box displays the total length of time your presenta-tion took and asks if you want to record and use the new slide timings in a slide show. Choose **Yes**, if you want each slide to advance after the allocated time.

◆ The slide timings are displayed in Slide Sorter view.

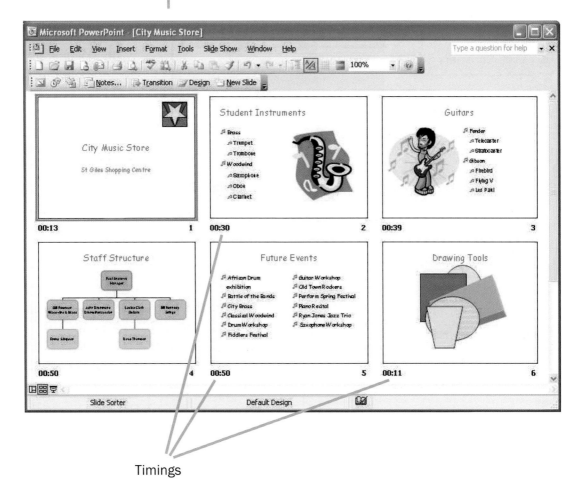

Timings

Summary Slide

You can get PowerPoint to automatically produce a Summary Slide for your presentation. The Summary Slide is created by taking the Titles from the slides that you select, and listing them on a slide that is placed in front of the selected slides. PowerPoint will generate as many Summary Slides as is necessary to list the Slide Titles from all selected slides.

> ## Tip
> Do not select your Title slide when creating a summary slide.

1 Select the slides to use in the Summary Slide

   For adjacent slides, select the first, hold down [**Shift**] and click on the last slide

   Or

   For non-adjacent slides, hold down [**Ctrl**] and click on each of the slides

2 Click  the **Summary Slide** tool on the Slide Sorter toolbar

2 Click Summary Slide

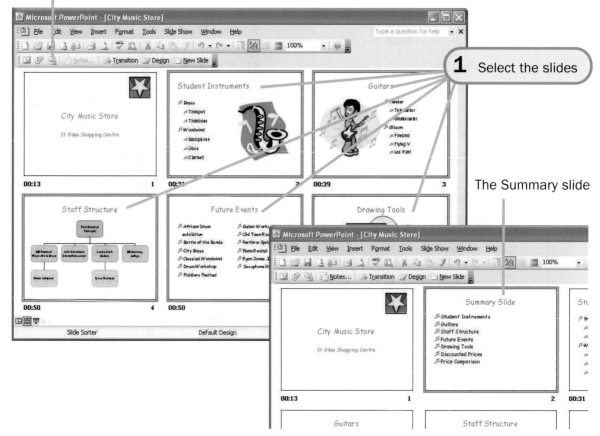

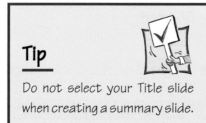

1 Select the slides

The Summary slide

Basic steps

1 Select the slide(s) to add a transition effect to

2 Click the **Slide Transition** tool ⟨📑 Transition⟩

3 Select an effect (it will be previewed if AutoPreview is turned on at the bottom of the task pane)

4 Set the **Speed**, and select a **Sound** if wanted

5 Set an **Advance** option (usually **On mouse click**)

6 Click ⟨Apply to All Slides⟩

7 Click ⟨▶ Play⟩ to see the effect on the selected slide in Slide Sorter view

Or

8 Click ⟨🖵 Slide Show⟩ to display the slide and effect in Slide Show view.

9 Close the task pane when you have specified your requirements

A transition is an effect used between slides during the slide show. The default option is that No Transition is set, but there are several interesting alternatives that you might find effective. Experiment with the Transition options until you discover those best suited to your presentation.

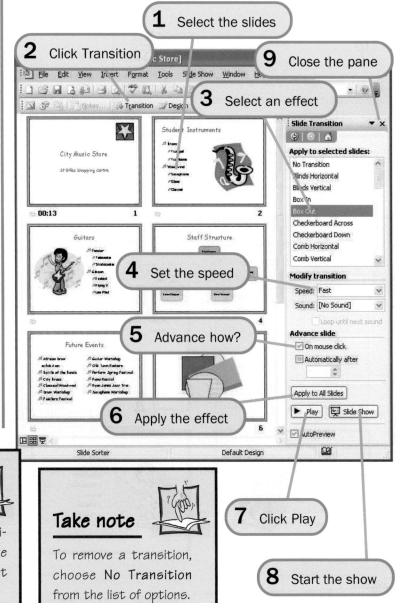

1 Select the slides
2 Click Transition
9 Close the pane
3 Select an effect
4 Set the speed
5 Advance how?
6 Apply the effect
7 Click Play
8 Start the show

Take note

If a transition is set, a transition icon appears below the slide in Slide Sorter view. Click on it to see the transition effect.

Take note

To remove a transition, choose No Transition from the list of options.

Animation schemes

If you have several bullet points listed on your slide, you could try building the slide up during the presentation, rather than presenting the whole list at once. This effect is achieved by adding an Animation Scheme to the slide.

Tip

Don't add too many transition and animation effects to your slides! They should add interest, but can easily become overpowering.

Basic steps

1 Click [Design] the **Design** tool

2 Select **Animation Schemes** on the **Slide Design** task pane

3 Select the slide(s) that you wish to animate

4 Pick an effect from the list

5 Click [Apply to All Slides]

6 Close the task pane when you have specified your requirements

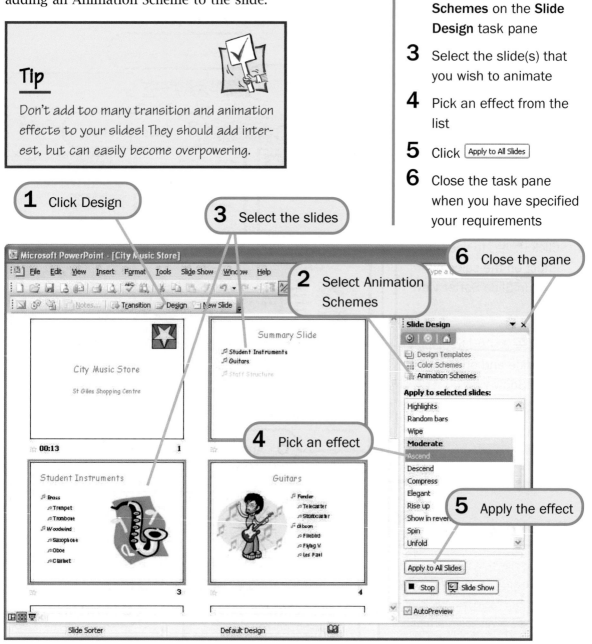

Exercises

A: City Music Store

1 Open the City Music Store presentation file.

2 Add some notes to slides 2 (Student Instruments), 4 (Staff Structure) and 9 (Price Comparison).

3 Hide slide 7 (the one with WordArt on it).

4 In Slide Sorter view, select all slides and add a Transition effect to the selected slides.

5 Select slide 2 and choose an Animation Scheme for it.

6 Create a Summary Slide after the Title Slide for all slides except slide 7.

7 Practise your presentation using the Rehearse Timings feature.

8 Save and close your file.

B: Westside Sports

1 Open the Westside Sports presentation file.

2 Add some notes to slides 2 (Children's Classes), 4 (Class Numbers) and 7 (Coaching Staff).

3 Hide Slide 6 (the one with WordArt on it).

4 Give each slide a Transition effect.

5 Select slide 2 (Children's Classes) and slide 5 (Activities on offer) and choose an Animation Scheme for them.

6 Move slide 5 (Coaching Staff) and put it in front of slide 2 (Children's Classes).

7 Create a Summary Slide after your Title Slide for all slides except slide 6.

8 Copy your Summary Slide to the end of the presentation.

9 Practice your presentation using Rehearse Timings.

10 Save and close your file.

C: Creatures of the Deep

1 Open the Creatures of the Deep presentation file.

2 Add some notes to slide 2 (Administrative Staff) and slide 7 (Latest sightings).

3 Hide slide 7.

4 Give each slide a Transition effect.

5 Select slides 3 and 4 and choose an Animation scheme for them.

6 Move slide 2 (Admin Staff) to the end of the presentation.

7 Create a Summary Slide after the Title Slide for all slides except slide 7.

8 Copy your Summary Slide to the end of the presentation.

9 Practise your presentation using the Rehearse Timings feature.

10 Save and close your file.

8 Presenting a show

Print Preview

Before you give a slide show, you may want to make printouts for your own use, or for your audience. You can print:

◆ Slides - onto paper or overhead transparencies, one slide per page.

◆ Handouts - miniatures of your slides, printed 2, 3, 4, 6 or 9 to the page.

◆ Notes Pages - each printed page has a slide miniature, together with any notes that you have made as prompts.

◆ Outline - containing only the text of each slide, to show the structure of the presentation.

Basic steps

1 Click the **Preview** tool  on the Standard toolbar

Or

2 Open the **File** menu and choose **Preview**

The Preview toolbar is displayed with your slide

Print Preview toolbar

Print Preview		
Previous Page		Displays previous page
Next Page		Displays next page
Print	Print...	Displays the Print dialog box
Print What	Print What: Slides	Slides, handouts, notes pages or Outline
Zoom	83%	Select a preset level from the list or type a value
Orientation		Options available for handouts only

Options	Options ▾	Options include
		   Header and Footer
		   Color/Grayscale
		   Scale to Fit paper
		   Frame Slides
		   Print Hidden Slides
		   Print Order – sets the print order for handouts

Close	Close	Closes the preview window
Help		Displays Print Preview Help dialog box

Basic steps

Print

- To display the Print dialog box

1 Choose **Print** from the **File** menu

Or

2 Click `🖨 Print...` on the Print Preview toolbar

- **Print selection**

3 Specify the slides that you wish to print in the **Slides** field

4 Click `Preview` to preview your work before you print it

5 Click `OK`

Many of the options that can be specified in Print Preview, can also be specified in the Print dialog box. In this box you can also specify the slides that you wish to print by entering their numbers in the Print range area.

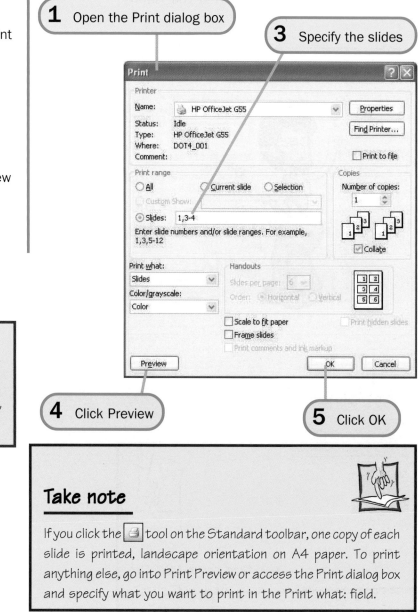

1 Open the Print dialog box

3 Specify the slides

4 Click Preview

5 Click OK

Tip

It's always best to preview your work before printing.

Take note

If you click the 🖨 tool on the Standard toolbar, one copy of each slide is printed, landscape orientation on A4 paper. To print anything else, go into Print Preview or access the Print dialog box and specify what you want to print in the Print what: field.

Viewing a show

You can run your slide show at any time to check how your presentation is progressing. During the slide show, each slide fills the whole of your computer screen.

After the last slide has been viewed, you are returned to the view you were in when you started your show.

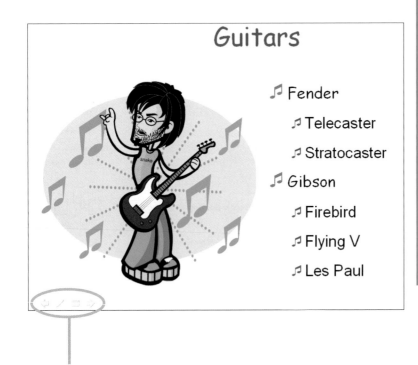

Slide navigation buttons

- **To start your Slide Show from slide 1**

1 Press [**F5**]

- **To start your Slide Show from any slide**

2 Select the slide you want to start from (in Normal or Slide Sorter view)

3 Click  the **Slide Show (from current slide)** icon to the left of the horizontal scroll bar

Or

4 Press [**Shift**]-[**F5**]

Each time you click the left mouse button, the next slide in your presentation will be displayed

Take note

You can exit your Slide Show at any time by pressing [Esc].

Tip

Use Slide Show view together with Slide Sorter view when experimenting with Transition and Animation effects. You can then check that the options you choose are having the desired effect.

Slide Navigation

- **To move to the next slide**

1 Click the mouse button

Or

Press **[PageDown]**

Or

Click 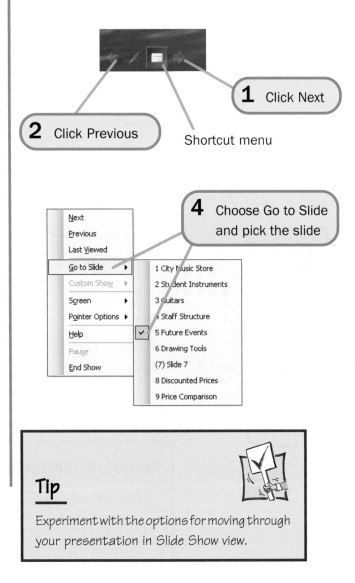 at the bottom left of the screen

- **To go to the previous slide**

2 Click 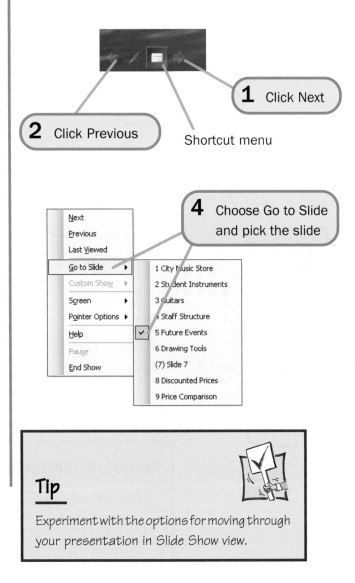, or right-click anywhere on the screen, then choose **Previous** from the pop-up menu

Or

Press **[PageUp]**

Or

Click 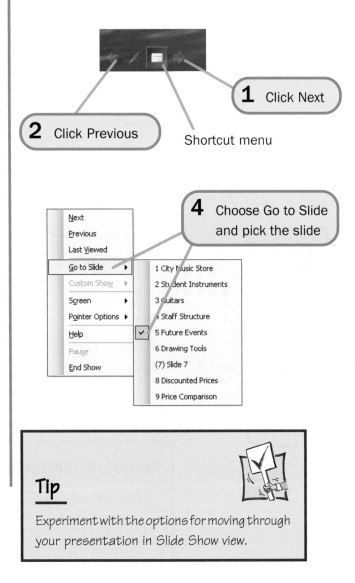 at the bottom left of the screen

- **To go to a specific slide**

3 Type the slide number and press **[Enter]**

Or

4 Click the menu icon 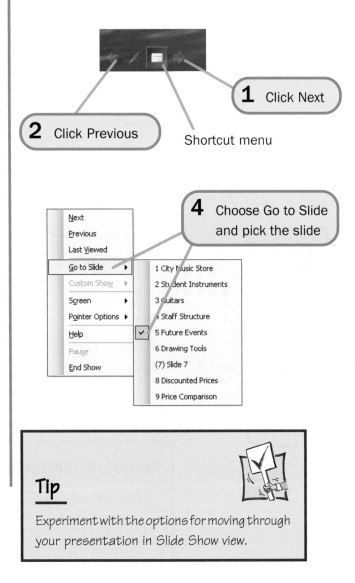, or right-click on the screen, choose **Go to Slide**, and select the slide from the pop-up menu

When presenting your slide show, there are several ways to navigate your way through your slides. You will normally want to progress through your slides from beginning to end, but there are also ways to backtrack, or jump from one slide to another. Experiment with the options and use the ones you find easiest.

1 Click Next

2 Click Previous

Shortcut menu

4 Choose Go to Slide and pick the slide

| Next |
| Previous |
| Last Viewed |
| Go to Slide ▶ |
| Custom Show ▶ |
| Screen ▶ |
| Pointer Options ▶ |
| Help |
| Pause |
| End Show |

1 City Music Store
2 Student Instruments
3 Guitars
4 Staff Structure
✓ 5 Future Events
6 Drawing Tools
(7) Slide 7
8 Discounted Prices
9 Price Comparison

Tip

Experiment with the options for moving through your presentation in Slide Show view.

111

Pens and arrows

You can quickly change your mouse pointer to a pen so that you can annotate a slide, or draw something on your 'blackboard' or 'whiteboard' (see next page). Pen and arrow options are in the pen pop-up menu.

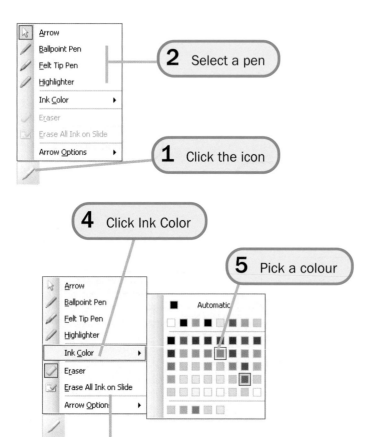

2 Select a pen

1 Click the icon

4 Click Ink Color

5 Pick a colour

9 Click Erase All Ink

Basic steps

1 Click ⬚ to display the pen pop-up menu

■ **To 'draw' on the screen**

2 Select a pen – Ballpoint, Felt Tip or Highlighter

3 Click and drag to draw

■ To specify an ink colour

4 Select **Ink Color**

5 Click on an ink colour

■ **To return to the Arrow mouse pointer**

6 Select the **Arrow** option

■ **To erase annotations from the screen**

7 Choose **Eraser**

8 Click on the area you wish to erase

■ **To erase all drawing**

9 Choose **Erase All Ink on Slide**

Keyboard shortcuts for pens and arrows:

[Ctrl]-[P] *changes the pointer to the Ballpoint pen*

[Ctrl]-[A] *changes the pointer to the Arrow*

[Ctrl]-[E] *changes the pointer to the Eraser*

Blackout and Whiteout

1 Press **[B]** to Blackout your screen

Or

Press **[W]** to Whiteout your screen

2 Press **[B]** or **[W]** again to return to the slide show

There may be times when you wish to blackout (or whiteout) your screen, so as not to distract your audience as you demonstrate or show them something.

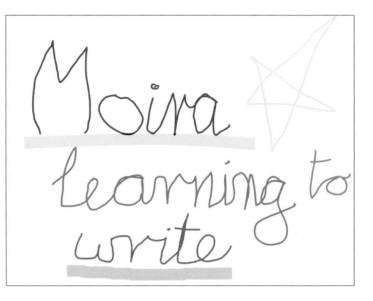

Slide Show Help

During the slide show:	OK
'N', left click, space, right or down arrow, enter, or page down	Advance to the next slide
'P', backspace, left or up arrow, or page up	Return to the previous slide
Number followed by Enter	Go to that slide
'B' or '.'	Blacks/Unblacks the screen
'W' or ','	Whites/Unwhites the screen
'A' or '='	Show/Hide the arrow pointer
'S' or '+'	Stop/Restart automatic show
Esc, Ctrl+Break, or '-'	End slide show
'E'	Erase drawing on screen
'H'	Go to hidden slide
'T'	Rehearse - Use new time
'O'	Rehearse - Use original time
'M'	Rehearse - Advance on mouse click
Hold both buttons down for 2 secs.	Return to first slide
Ctrl+P	Change pointer to pen
Ctrl+A	Change pointer to arrow
Ctrl+E	Change pointer to eraser
Ctrl+H	Hide pointer and button
Ctrl+U	Automatically show/hide arrow
Right mouse click	Popup menu/Previous slide
Ctrl+S	All Slides dialog
Ctrl+T	View task bar
Ctrl+M	Show/Hide ink markup

When practising your slide show, press [F1] to display the Slide Show Help dialog box.

Experiment with the options and use them as necessary when delivering a presentation.

Exercises

A: City Music Store

1   Open the City Music Store presentation file.

2   Print Preview your file and set it up to print 6 slides to the page (handouts).

3   Add the file name to the header area and your name to the footer area, then print the first page of slides.

4   Display or select slide 6 in your file (depending on whether you are in Normal or Slide Sorter view).

5   Press [F5] – notice that the slide show starts at slide 1.

6   Click the left mouse button to move through the first three slides.

7   Press [Esc] to exit the slide show.

8   Display or select slide 4 in your file.

9   Click the **Slide Show from Current Slide** icon (bottom left) – notice that the slide show starts from slide 4.

10 Experiment moving forwards and backwards through the slides in your slide show.

11 Go to slide 2.

12 Using the felt pen option, draw a blue ring around the brass instruments.

13 Erase the annotation using your keyboard.

14 Exit your Slide Show and close your file.

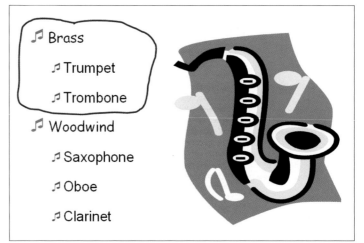

B: Westside Sports

1 Open the Westside Sports presentation file.

2 Print Preview the file and set it up to print 3 slides to a page.

3 Add the file name to the header area and your name to the footer area, then print the first page of slides.

4 Start the slide show from Slide 1.

5 Go directly to slide 5.

6 Use the Highlighter to highlight Badminton, Squash, Table Tennis and Tennis.

7 Remove the annotation from your slide.

8 Exit the slide show and close your file.

C: Creatures of the Deep

1 Open the Creatures of the Deep presentation file.

2 Print Preview your file and set it up to print 4 slides to the page.

3 Add your name to the page footer and print page 1 only.

4 Start your slide show from slide 1 and work through the slides using your keyboard.

5 Ann Grant starts in November – annotate the slide to indicate this.

6 Remove the annotation from your slide.

7 Use the pop-up menu to jump to the slide 'Latest Sightings'.

8 Exit the Slide Show and close your file.

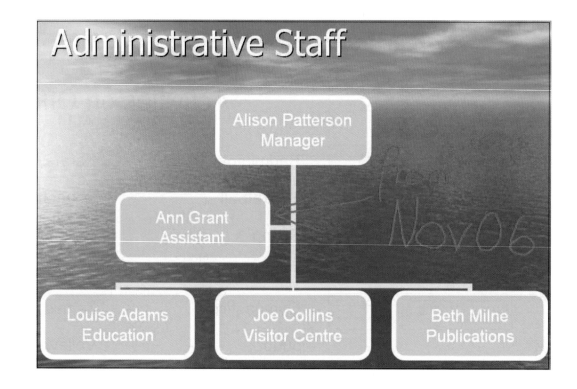

Index